How to Jump From a Ferris Wheel and Land On Your Feet, Vol. III

Ten Women
Ten Chapters
Ten Stories

www.candalysepublishing.com
Candalyse Publishing * New York

First Edition

ISBN: 978-0-9817112-0-1
ISBN: 0-9817112-0-0

Published in the United States of America

Candalyse Publishing
Bethel, New York 12778

Also Available in the Ferris Wheel Series:

**How to Jump From a Ferris Wheel and
Land on Your Feet**

ISBN: 978-0-9798217-9-0
Foreword by Fran Briggs

**How to Jump From a Ferris Wheel and
Land on Your Feet, Vol. II**

ISBN: 978-0-9802275-6-7
Foreword by Yvonne Pierre

Foreword

Travel on ten journeys, with ten strong women, who will teach you how to jump from a Ferris wheel and land on your feet each time you fall.

You will be empowered, motivated, and moved by each story.

These are powerful testimonies of ten women who have experienced life on ten different levels, and fought their way out of situations that most people would not have made it through.

These women are Eagles that soar with struggles, who slipped, looked up, remembered, were lost and then found, hit rock bottom, reached back, pressed forward, and thrived through every circumstance. You will learn how to remove fear from your life, succeed beyond your belief system, have no more excuses, and learn to live your dreams.

Simply put, your life will never be the same.

Tawana Williams
Motivational Speaker

Author of <u>Unarmed, But Dangerous</u>
www.tawanawilliams.com

Table of Contents

Through The Storm

Melissa R. Martin

I recall walking around the house in total shock as I managed to get showered and dressed. Black? I had to wear black, I thought to myself, as I glanced in the mirror once more. Tears streamed down my face as the events of the past week came flooding in. I had filed for divorce from my husband of eighteen years and backed it up with a restraining order. He moved in with his parents who lived next door, which provided me little sense of security. I kept the doors locked and jumped at every little sound. And I waited. I waited for his next drunken tirade. I waited for him to break down the door.... again. I waited for him to hold me captive with a gun to my head. I actually waited for him to end my life. No one seemed to listen, or did not care... but I was fighting tooth and nail to get out. Sometimes I felt like I was the only person in the world who could see what he was doing to me.

My children didn't understand, and blamed me, which I found so heartbreaking. So many times I had stood between them and the blows from their father. So many times I had taken the brunt of his anger, to protect them... and yet, they cried for him, wanted him back home, looked at me with disappointing eyes.... like I was to blame for our broken home. My heart was breaking beneath the weight of it all, and then the call came.

My father, who had recently had a stroke, had taken a turn for the worse, and the family was called to the hospital. It was almost more than I could bear. I remember feeling numb as I walked through the hospital doors. I can't even recall how I got there. But as I stood in the entrance to his room, I felt my legs go weak beneath me.

The man who had been my strength and pushed me forward, who had told me never to give up, was lying in a hospital bed on life support with a raging fever. The family was called in so they could slowly turn off the ventilator. My mother was in tears, telling my father that she was sorry; she was the one who had to sign to have the ventilator turned off. To this day, I think she still blames herself for giving up on him, even when the doctors said there was no chance of his survival.

Inside the room, I held the hand of the man who had watched me take my first breath of life. I cried like a baby as I watched him take his last. There was so much pain; I didn't know where to turn. I kissed his brow as a final, single tear ran down his cheek. Perhaps, it was his way of saying goodbye. Perhaps, there was something he had wanted to say, but could not. I walked away with incredible sadness hanging over me. I don't even recall how or when I made it home that night, but someone else was very much aware of my comings and goings.

Home alone, it really hit me!

The silence within the four walls around me was deafening. The past few hours kept running through my mind. There was a thump at the back door, and then there was a reality check. It was him! My soon-to-be ex-husband had come calling. How could he do this? I had just lost my father! After four beers, he became void of any feelings whatsoever. I was guessing he was starting on his seventh!

However, in the midst of what would usually cause me terror, I strangely felt nothing! Everything was a blur. The fear was even gone! At that very moment, I didn't care what he was going to do to me. I just knew that I was tired of running. I was sick and tired of being the victim, and so I stood. Through every accusation, every filthy word, and each pull of my hair - I stood.

When he passed out in mid-swing, I was still standing....

The next day I was dressing for my father's visitation service and looking into the mirror with a beautiful black eye, a cracked cheekbone, and a fair-sized laceration on my face. I cried. Partly because of how I looked, partly because it had happened again, and partly because I was saying goodbye to the greatest father and best friend I ever had.

Needless to say, people walked by and gave the pitiful glances at the funeral home. No one asked what happened. They didn't have to, or didn't want to. I'm not sure which. I sat alone in my grief and embarrassment as the world said goodbye to my father. Deep inside, I knew that life would never be the same and that I was literally going to have to get tough, or die.

We buried my father on the hill behind his house on a cold, windy, November day. I walked away from his grave knowing I would never see him again or even be able to place flowers on his grave. In a crowd, and yet still so utterly alone, I silently said farewell to the life I had known.

I went home, locked my doors, and began packing. Some people would call it running away. I called it saving myself. The cold wind was still blowing as I stepped onto that big, black train. I found my seat beside the window, wrapped myself in a blanket, and never looked back.

In my travels, I grew stronger, more confident. I found a wonderful friend who took me in and later became my husband. The nightmares came less often, I stopped jumping at every little sound, and I could leave the doors unlocked!

I found peace, joy, love, and happiness beyond measure some two thousand miles away from the man who once caused me pain. I still have things I need to work on. I still hurt when old memories call, and I still miss the loved ones I left behind. I wish I could hold them, laugh with them, place flowers on Daddy's grave, but I traveled this far to find safety and the faith to make it through.

My soul mate is always near to share in the smiles, wipe away the tears, and just hold me when I'm hurting. Nevertheless, I am a long way from that pitiful, beat-down woman that sat in a corner of a funeral home mourning the loss of her father while the town whispered and looked the other way.

Healing has come, healing continues, and God has brought me through the storm.

 **Melissa R. Martin,** author of **Trapped in My Pen**, was born in Wise, Virginia, the fifth of six children, to Albert and Christene Mullins. People Writing from the heart and from past experiences, she feels that her writing is a gift from God and that He has given her the strength to keep faith in the face of hardship. Melissa has lived through many wonderful times, met countless precious people, and has seen some absolutely beautiful places- and thus, she writes to share, to uplift, to heal, and to express her gratitude to those who have touched her life in positive ways. To the ones who struggle with the trials of life, Melissa's hope is that they can find comfort within the lines she so carefully penned with love....

Contact Melissa on the web at

http://www.myspace.com/missyvirginiahoney

http://www.shoutlife.com/profile_view.cfm?uid=91880

http://www.authorsden.com/melissarmartin

http://candalysepublishing.com/melissa_martin.html

http://trappedinmypen.faithweb.com/index.html

You Can't Hang with Ducks, if You Are an Eagle

Tawana Williams

An eagle in flight is magnificent. Its wings allow it to soar above the earth with majestic power. The scene makes you stop whatever you are doing and watch. Watching the eagle fly reminds me of God's power.

The eagle is so powerful that it can even soar above an approaching storm. It catches the wind by the tail and then rides the air currents, much like a surfer who catches a good wave. It does not fear. It does not panic. It only watches and waits until just the right moment and then aligns itself with the coming force of nature. Then it rides, glides, and soars.

Just imagine that same eagle without wings. Without its wings, the eagle would be powerless. It would not be able to surf the storm, soar above the earth, and we would miss the sight of him in flight. Without wings, the eagle would also starve. Its ability to fly high above the earth and search out his prey would be lost. The eagle would not be able to swoop down and catch in its claws the prey it needs for survival. Without its wings, this magnificent bird of prey would die.

Like that eagle, we have all been created to soar. Most of us came into the world with arms, legs, a functioning mind, and a healthy body. Like that eagle, we each have the chance to soar above our life's storms and catch the tail of our dreams and feel the wind of our vision. With arms outspread, we each wait for our chance to catch a wave and soar.

But my story is a bit different. As you read it, my prayer is that you will see that eagles can learn to fly, even without wings. I pray that my story will encourage you to live without excuses and even if your wings get broken, make the attempt to fly. I believe that if you will try, then you will live. If you don't try, then like the eagle without wings, your dreams will surely die.

My prayer is that you will see that God has given you many gifts and you can do so many things to bring Him glory. I encourage you to look beyond your boundaries, live your life to its fullest potential, and soar about your life's storms with power.

I was born without arms to a mother who told me, "... there is nothing that you cannot do," and Grandma Rogers told me that, "You must not have needed arms, because God didn't give them to you." Armed with those words in my heart, I knew that I was destined for greatness. After struggling for many years with adversities, low or no self-esteem, and identity crises, tragedy struck in 1981 when I was a senior in high school. A so-called friend introduced me to crack cocaine.

Nothing and no one could have ever prepared me for the turn that my life was about to take. I said to myself after taking that first hit, "I can handle this." That was the biggest *lie* that I had ever told. Crack became my lover, my best friend; my everything. I did not care about my family, my mate. But, the worst part of my addiction was that I didn't care about *me*. I allowed crack to put me in a place where I hated my reflection in the mirror. I did things for crack I had never thought that I would do. I stole for it, lied for it, had unprotected sex for it; I was completely out of control.

During my ten-year addiction, I was faced with some life-altering tragedies. I was gang-raped when my home was invaded, raped by my step-dad, experienced abortion, and motherhood. After hitting rock bottom in 1991, I cried out to God for help. I said, "God, I need you to do one or the other; either kill me in my sleep, or deliver me from crack." God answered my prayers instantly. I was delivered from my addiction in my sleep.

I awakened *brand-new*. I had finally realized my greatness, my purpose, and my gifts. I was free... I began to do things that others said were impossible for me to do without arms. I took care of my baby; I fed her, dressed her, and bathed her, even without arms. They didn't know it, but they were challenging me to do more, to do bigger and better things.

Doors began to open for me; I had arrived. I became a Motivational Speaker. My husband, Toby, and I were traveling all over this country changing lives with my message of hope and inspiration. I connected with Les Brown, and he became my mentor. We went to schools, churches, prisons, day care centers, nursing homes, and corporations being a blessing. We did this for more than nine and a half years, free of charge. It has been said that, "when it's your passion and purpose, you'll do it for free, and you'll do it so well that people will begin to pay you to do it." That is what happened for me.

Many times, we were promised to be paid, and when we arrived, we were not paid. I did not allow that to cause me to stop. I did not allow that to discourage me. Sometimes it did get to me, and that will happen to you, too. I have found that things in life will make you bitter or make you better. A man once said that, "... bitterness is like drinking poison, and expecting someone else to get sick."

I have learned something from all those experiences, and it has brought me to where I am right now. If you want something, you've got to be willing to pay the price. You have got to be willing to face whatever comes your way.

Life will test you, and it has a way of finding out where you live even though you didn't give out your address. No test, no testimony... You've got to press your way through, you've got to be determined to make it, no matter what.

I can't tell you all the moments of frustration, disappointments, and set-backs that I've had. The trials and errors that I have gone through just trying to do something new, trying to learn something different. While trying to do something that I was told I could not do, I became so determined, so driven, that I just refused to give up, and I did it.

You will find such determination in yourself, too. Decide to look at yourself and your dreams. Whatever it is that you want to do - just do it. If you can get some help, that is great, but the major key to your success or failure in life is you. Do it yourself. Set standards for yourself. Stop going through life just complaining about things.

Some of us go through each day signing up to be volunteer victims, working on jobs that we hate, doing just enough to get by. We've got into the habit of being mediocre; no, that's no way to live. Stop accepting life as it is; if your life is not what you want it to be, then you, and only you, have the power to change it. You are the keeper of your mind, and the captain of your ship.

When I was told that I could not get a job, I decided to create my own job. I am the CEO of my company, I write my own checks, and I am my own boss. I decided to become a Speaker. I don't sit back and wait for things to happen for me; I make things happen for me. I believe that we all were created with greatness on the inside. It's up to each individual to dig deep within herself to find it; it is in there.

So, what legacy will you leave behind? What statue will be erected in your name? What mark will you leave for the world to know that you made a difference? I know; that is something to think about.

My legacy will be, she was "Unarmed, But Dangerous in every aspect of her life. She used every gift that God gave her. She Lived Full and Died Empty..."

I am Tawana Williams, your messenger of hope and inspiration. Hold onto these words until we meet again. I know that I will; even without arms.

Tawana Williams *is a Motivational Speaker, Mentor, and Author. Please visit Tawana on the web at www.tawanawilliams.com to order your autographed copy of "Unarmed, But Dangerous"... It is a life changing experience. To be mentored by Tawana Williams and some of the most prominent speakers, trainers, and teachers in the world, please visit www.unarmedbutdangerous2.mentorsclub.com*

Tawana and her husband, Toby.

I Lost Her

Makeisha Williams

By the time I was eighteen-years-old, I had overcome so many obstacles; lost people that I loved in so many different ways. I had lived so many places, through no choice of my own. When things seemed as if they could not get any worse, my world was turned upside down and inside out, all at once.

People deal with situations differently, especially death. I have always dealt with death extremely well until the death of one of my high school friends. After dealing with the deaths of my grandparents, I could not deal with any more. Then the untimely death of my friend happened.

It was hard enough letting her into my world because of past hurts and multiple betrayals, but befriending her was different. Losing her through death felt as if I had lost my sister, my best friend, and most of all, it was as if a piece of my heart was lost and could never be replaced. When I first started dealing with the deaths of people who were near and dear to my heart, I had to come to the realization that death is final- once you are dead and gone, there is no way to come back from that state.

It has been six and a half long years since her death. After six and a half years, people might think that I would be over the death of one of my dearest high school friends. The reality, however, is that I am far from over it. I came to this realization while dealing with a personal storm. I placed a stuffed bear that she had given me onto my bed and started to talk to the bear, as if the bear was she. Once I understood what I was doing, I lay on my bed, and cried in disbelief.

All that pain that I thought I had let go of was still eating away at my heart each day. My friend was so special to me because throughout our friendship, she became my sister. We did nearly everything together from singing in church to working the same summer job. If I cried, I could trust and believe that she would be there to cry with me and to tell me that everything would be okay. If it had not been for her, I would not know half of the church songs that I know today.

I can still remember the last time that I saw her. It was the first semester of senior year of high school. I did not have exams on the last day before Christmas break began. I got up anyway and dressed because I was to leave to see my family. For some reason, this particular morning was different from other mornings because I walked to the door of the dorm. As I watched her go to the bus stop, I yelled out, "See you later! I love you. I will see you when I make it to ECU."

She responded, "Make me proud." Four days later, I got the dreaded call that she had been killed in a car accident. I was in shock, yet I could not cry. After I returned home, it finally hit me that I would never see my friend again. There would be no more clowning in the school cafeteria, no more chilling before class in the common area because it was all over. My mind was consumed with terrible thoughts. All I could think of was why I never had the chance to really say goodbye. I felt that I should have been there to save her.

At the time, I wished that I could have traded in my life for her life because I had made it to the age of eighteen and she had not. I wanted to bring her back to her family. While dealing with the initial shock of her death I found myself walking around in a trance and not being able to tell one day from the next. I started to fall short in areas that I never would have imagined falling short in. I went from being a caring soul to being a beast. The beast in me would lash out at any and everyone who said something that I did not like.

I could not grasp reality. Food became my refuge. If the food was not nailed down, I ate it because I thought that food could help me to deal with my pain. Eventually, I started to come around to see people. I started to cover the pain that I was going through, focusing more on things that could keep me busy so that I would not have to think about the loss.

My heart is still torn from her death and at times I feel like I have failed her because I never finished ECU. I changed a lot about myself after losing her. When I lost her I lost my heart. My heart hardened. I toughened up and refused to let anyone get close to me. Although I have met new people and made new friends, I did not think that I would ever let anyone get that close to me anymore.

Letting Go

I came to the realization that I was still grieving over her and I decided that it was time to let her go. I prayed long and hard on the situation because I knew that letting her go would be the best thing for me emotionally, as well as giving me the opportunity to move on with my life.

Praying really helped a lot. It gave me the strength that I need to go on even though it has only been a few months since this revelation. I have begun to let people into my life and to share the love that I used to give before I hardened my heart. I know that we will be able to see each other one day while singing in the Heavenly Choir together. I feel her presence as she is watching down on me. No one will be able to take her place in my heart but it is time for me to move on.

I know that she is proud of me no matter what I do. Having the understanding that she will be proud no matter which school of higher learning I get my degree from keeps my heart at peace. Although she is gone away from this earth, today I know that I can succeed in every way.

I am at peace knowing that she was placed in my life for a reason and that God loaned her to me for a season. I am now celebrating the life that she led and the joy that she brought to my heart. I love my life and I am living it to the fullest now, as I did before.

Makeisha Williams was born and raised in North Carolina but now resides in Maryland. She was raised in the foster care system. After leaving the foster care system, Makeisha began her college career in Social Work but after finding her passion for the law and justice, she switched her major to Criminal Justice. Makeisha hopes to pursue law school to practice Criminal and Family Law. Makeisha Williams is the Co-founder of a social organization named Dedicated Individuals Victoriously Achieving Success (D.I.V.A.S) that caters to the plus-sized community.

Through The Fire

Judith A. Battiste

According to <u>Webster's New World Dictionary,</u> *fear* is defined as anxiety caused by real or possible danger, pain, apprehension, or concern.

According to a sixteen-year-old girl, fear knows that in nine months she will be a mother to the little life that is growing inside of her.

For three months, I kept a secret. A secret that became so tangible it stuck out like a pregnant woman's belly, pun intended! I was always what one would consider an "ideal child." I stayed out of trouble, got A's and B's in school, and even had my own job and bank account. Of course, there was the occasional blown curfew, sassing back to the folks, and refusal of doing chores, but overall what more could a parent ask for?

Now, imagine you are that "ideal child" with the pressure on your shoulders to maintain that image. No doubt it would be pretty apprehensive letting your parents down, especially if you have to tell them that their baby girl is expecting a baby girl!

As the middle child of three children, I was supposed to be the responsible and mature kid. It was expected that I should learn from my older sister's mistakes and be a role model for my younger brother. So when I discovered that I was pregnant just eleven months after my seventeen-year-old sister gave birth to my niece, I felt anxiety, caused by a very real and possible danger.

I felt fear!

Week after week, I gained pound after pound, but the weight on my conscience weighed heavier than that of my expanding waistline.

"I could not have a baby right now," I told myself. I was almost out of high school, working a part-time job at a local movie theatre, and was still taking advice from my mom, my sister, peers, Brenda and Brandon Walsh on Beverly Hills 90210, and the self-help columns in Seventeen Magazine!

"Do I keep my baby and raise her as an unwed high school drop-out, rely on welfare and government assisted programs, work three jobs to make ends meet, and eat meals from local shelters?" I asked.

"Or do I abort my baby and continue down the easy road of a care-free college bound teenaged girl?" My future looked very bleak. Whoever opts for the road less traveled? Who stares adversity in the face with open arms, almost certain to see their impending demise? Who? But me!

The Reality Check

At one thirty on May 7th, 2000, I gave birth to a six-pound two-ounce baby girl named, Alyse Danielle. As beautiful and precious as she was, the reality of motherhood hit me the night I missed Prom. I had a two-week-old baby at home with colic and jaundice; there would be no corsages, tiaras, and limo rides for me. I was a mother now and mothers do not go to Prom when their baby has a fever. Mothers do not eat franks and drink punch at weekend barbecues when they have no babysitter. They do not go to Cancun for Spring Break or even to the movies with their boyfriends if their baby is teething!

Instead, mothers get full-time jobs and go to school in hopes of eventually getting a better job. They wake up early and go to bed late; yes, my future looked very bleak, indeed.

Although I was only seeing the world through the pessimistic glasses I loved to wear, I was, by no means, on the road less traveled. To my surprise, I became acquainted with many young girls in my school that were single mothers, too. They were raising their children, working, and going to school, like me.

I began to see things differently. It gave me inspiration to pummel through what I thought was a hindrance to my bigger picture. What was my bigger picture? Who knows, but what I did know was what society told me: unwed teenaged girls do not have kids, and if they do, they will not succeed. Luckily for me I had love and support from my grandmother, amongst other figures in my life. I moved in with her after Alyse was just six months old. Granny is a very strong, old-fashioned, and tough woman. I thought for sure that I would live up to society's standard living with her, but she proved me wrong. She would often tell me, "Do not punish yourself by the mistakes of your past. You are young and you made mistakes; but, we all make mistakes." Granny was right. Just because I found myself in what seemed to be a difficult situation did not mean that I was doomed to fail.

Failure is non-performance of what is expected; I believe failure is only a mental constraint. Only you can decide whether you can fail or succeed at something. Salvator Dali once said, "The thermometer of success is merely the jealousy of the malcontents." But, who sets these standards that measure our successes against our supposed failures? So what, the statistics stand to reason that teen mothers are less likely to complete high school and that nearly 80% are more likely to end up on welfare. You have to distinguish between whether it is you that is the malcontent, or society. Often times, the only thing holding you back from something is yourself. If you allow yourself to buy into everything the media and society sells to you, then you will always be held back behind the malcontents.

Never let anyone determine your path and set limits to your success. I have not.

I am currently the Assistant Branch Manager at a national bank. I endured a rigorous training program to obtain my NYS Life Insurance license that allows me to sell investment products. This not only increases my earnings potential, but also expounds on my growth potential within my field.

It is still a struggle, but I feel like I have no limits. Over the years, I have learned to embrace my single-parenthood. It has been eight years and I have yet to finish college, but I am not discouraged. I decided that it was a better decision for me to focus on my career, even at the cost of putting school on the back burner for a little bit. I hope in a few years that I will be able to use the skills that I have developed in the financial arena of banking, to open and manage a restaurant and live out my passion for cooking.

I have been able to use my experiences as a teenaged mother as guidance and not roadblocks towards my bigger picture. And, what is my bigger picture you ask? It is intangible to my many malcontents, but as tangible as a single, teenaged mother beating the odds; there is nothing bleak about that!

Judith A. Battiste was born New York in December 1982. She is the second of three children born to proud parents Miriam L. Jacobs and Gregoire Battiste. Judith has used her passion for writing to assist others to assert themselves and not be ashamed of their past choices but to use them as guideposts instead of roadblocks. Her eight-year-old daughter, Alyse Danielle Battiste, is a published author, writing and publishing her first children's book, <u>Super Sally's Fantastic Fun Day.</u> (2008 Candalyse Publishing)

I Remember

Teresa Bryant

I remember running as fast as I could. I could hear him close behind and I knew that with one wrong step he would have hold of me. In my hands was his loaded gun. I remember separating the gun and clip from each other and throwing the two in separate directions. I also remember that it was at that very same moment that he grabbed my hair and yanked me back; that it would have only taken but a moment for him to end my life.

When he was angry he was so very evil. I could look into his eyes and see nothing but blackness that you could see no end to. I remember waking up to him hitting me in the face and smiling while he did so. I remember the smell of his evil breath and how it excited him to hurt me. The more that he hurt me, the more he pranced when he walked. It was like every bruise and broken bone was a ribbon of accomplishment. He loved his work. He loved the fear that he saw in my eyes. It excited him to control me.

He could be trying to kill me one minute and the next he acted as though he was the victim. How easy it was for him to convince others that it was I who was nuts; that he had not been doing anything, and that he could never do the things that I accused him of. After awhile, I just stopped trying to convince anyone and accepted the fact that he was in control. I became too tired to even cry.

He took such pride with his sexual abuse, too. My neighbors could hear me screaming from inside our home. How he destroyed my insides and how the surgeons had to remove a quarter of each of my ovaries. How when I got to the hospital, severe internal bleeding caused me to be given two transfusions just to keep me alive. I also remember denying that he had hurt me, telling everyone that I did not know how the injuries happened; I awoke in pain, and called 911 for help.

He actually broke both of his hands and was in a cast the next day from doing so. He broke his bones while breaking mine. He acted as though he was the victim, crying and begging for forgiveness. I remember forgiving him because I was just too tired to care. I was extremely mentally drained by then to do anything but breathe. I was his to do with as he pleased.

When he knew that others were catching on to what he was doing, he suddenly moved us away. He isolated me from those who might be able to take away his control. He made sure that I had no strength, no way to change what was happening. I remember wishing that death would come, so that I could escape his control and not feel any more pain. I was so ashamed by then for allowing this to go on that I did not believe that I could live without him. The thought of leaving and starting over alone was just way too much work. He had broken me, and he loved it.

One day, I had gone out to run some errands. While I was gone, he became enraged about something. When I returned, he was swinging in the hammock wearing this evil smile on his face. I could tell that something was wrong. As I walked past him, I noticed something in the bush beside the walkway. It was my dog. He had killed him with a hammer to the head. He did this because I was gone for too long.

He would tell me that it was I who caused him to act the way that he did. The smile that he wore that day still haunts me. The pleasure that he got from watching me die inside was all that he ever wanted.

In my lifetime, I have been in two abusive relationships. I was so ashamed that I had allowed this abuse to happen again. I actually began to believe that I deserved what was happening. That it really was I who caused the men to act the way that they did. I believed that I must be the type of person who made those who loved me go crazy; that I was somehow pushing them to the point that they had no control and I made them want to hurt me.

My abuser's children came to live with us. When they came to us, the baby girl was eleven-months-old and her brother was seven-years-old. They began to love me as if I was their biological mother, depending on me, and becoming my whole life. When he noticed that he could control me by using his children, he did so quite often. He would not hesitate to hurt his own son, scaring me nearly to death.

I knew that I needed to find a way to take back control of my life. I knew that if I did not, he was going to kill me one day. I could not just leave and let the children suffer because I was gone. By then I loved them like my own and would have done anything to make sure that they stayed safe.

This is when I decided that they only way to change things and to get us back to where there were others who cared for us was to make him lose all that he had. Slowly, he lost his job, then his home, then his vehicle, and everything else that he had. I forced him to return to where his relatives lived because he had no other choice.

He was angry all the time and the beatings got much worse. He was losing control. Typically, this is when the abuser becomes the most dangerous. His choices were being removed and I took the brunt of it.

I prepared the children for our separation. Seven years had passed from the time that they first came to live with us. Since the kids had come to live with us, I had always tucked them in at night. As I tucked them in, I always told them, "I love you up to the moon and down again, and around the world and back again." I told them that no matter where I was, when they looked up to the moon, I would be sending my love and when they missed me, the moon would reassure them that I loved them.

Freedom

The day that I walked away, I left with only my jacket and a flashlight. I walked away from all that I owned, all that I loved, and all that I feared. He only hurt me one more time after that, and he was put in jail for a few days. By the time that he got out, I was long gone.

I knew that when I left, I was never going to be able to see the children again. I knew that he would never allow it. I had no parental rights and could not legally do anything. I have never seen them again, although I have managed to check on them once by phone. Grandma said that Baby Girl was a straight A student. She was happy and well-adjusted. She told me that she was this way because of the things that I had taught her. She always looks up to the moon when she misses me. Her brother was a very different story. He became violent and very self-destructive, becoming like his father, having witnessed too much violence.

As I sit and ponder all that I have survived in my life, I get a warm feeling knowing that I came out the winner. I took back control of my life, and that is something that was very hard to do.

Domestic Violence affects everyone who is exposed to it. Children who grow up in these types of households are known to carry the behavior with them for life. Some abuse their families and some just live in fear. I would be lying if I told you that there were never any days that this did not still affect me because it does. When someone sneaks up behind me and catches me off guard, I *still* jump through the roof. I sometimes fear being outside at night.

I am a very strong person because of what I have been through. I have tried to make sure that I have worked through the things from my past. You cannot just bury these issues and never deal with them. You have to deal or they will never go away.

Forgiveness

Healing began when I started to forgive myself. As a result of soul-searching, I am no longer full of pain and anger like I once was. I have come to terms with the atrocities that happened to me, and I have calmness about me. I am very drawn to people and families in crisis. Someday, I will return to school and possibly take some counseling classes.

I did not realize for a long time just how much the past affected me, but it did. Since coming to terms with my past, I now live a very happy life. I started writing about a year ago and it has truly helped me. I have learned so much from everyone and everything that I have been through. I believe that knowledge is power. The more that you can learn from yourself and others, the more powerful you will be.

I now wake in the morning and look forward to life and all that I encounter. I can now say that when I shed a tear, it is because I am so very touched by the beautiful things in life and not because I am getting the hell beat out of me.

Don't give up. Even though it may seem as though there is no hope, there is. Know that somewhere in this world, I am fighting to bring awareness to all who will listen, and this is my promise to you.

I am proud to say that I am a survivor of Domestic Violence.

Teresa Bryant *is a forty-two-year-old mother from Elko, Nevada. She is engaged to be married to a wonderful man who has been supportive of her for ten years. Teresa is an advocate against Domestic Violence. Contact Teresa on the web at www.myspace.com/tresa69*

Slipping Through My Fingers –
Remembering My Aunt Pat

Dr. Naima Tonya Johnston

We think Aunt Pat died several days before Mother's Day; no one is really sure, but it was Mother's Day when we all found out. I was driving home from a special Mother's Day concert at a church in Brimfield, Ohio, 600 miles away from my entire family, when I got the call. With the breakthrough of modern technology and free nights and weekends from Sprint, I had spent a good deal of time on the phone laughing with my mother, and then chatting with my grandmother. The conversations made the three-hour trip back home in Fairborn, Ohio fly by fast; so fast that I barely noticed the cows and cornfields that dotted the landscape as I sped down Interstate 71.

Our family seemed to be gelling again; it was something I had been earnestly praying for; restoration and opportunity to witness to them about the love of Christ. We had seen each other a great deal over the last four months with weddings and special events. Although Aunt Pat had not made it home for my brother's wedding in March, we'd all been together for her daughter and my cousin, Kelly's, wedding in January.

It was my cousin Natachia who called and shattered my heart. My mom had found out shortly after hanging up with me, but not wanting to upset me 100 miles away from my home, driving alone in the middle of cow country Ohio, she was waiting to call me when she believed I had made it back to the small town of Fairborn. After several days of trying to get her mom on the phone, my cousin Kelly got worried and called the San Francisco Police. Officers dispatched to the house found my Aunt Pat dead. There was no autopsy since she was found at home and there was no sign of forced entry or foul play. She had been sick with diabetes and congestive heart failure, but no one really knew how sick she was.

I did not cry the entire way home; I didn't feel anything. All I knew was my Aunt Pat had died, and I was not sure if she had been a Christian. Aunt Pat had left the family and moved from the bustling and crowded streets of New York City to return to the sunny coastlines of California. California was where she was born and began her life, alone. It was in California where she died, alone. I had no idea if that aloneness followed her into eternity.

In situations like these, the details of a family saga are always vague. What I know for sure is that my Aunt was born on the West Coast to a mother who had no desire to raise her. There have been family whisperings that perhaps she had been in a children's home until her father, my great Uncle Al, who was my grandmother's brother, got leave from the Navy and snatched the squirming infant from a life of foster care and system causality.

Uncle Al directly deposited Aunt Pat into the arms of his mother and returned to the Service. She lived there until she was around twelve-years-old and Great Grandmother passed away. I was told that she was alone a lot. My grandmother, perhaps trying to show the motherless girl compassion and love, fed her, and fed her, and fed her some more.

Food became love, food became comfort, and Christ was never introduced as an answer to a deeper need. When Great Grandmother passed away, Aunt Pat went to live with my grandmother and transitioned from being a cousin to being a bratty little sister to my mother and her two brothers.

These are the stories I love to listen to. My Aunt Pat tormenting my father and mother as they took their first tentative steps into love and life. My Aunt Pat getting sent to sit on the bench to cool off when she got a little too sassy with my grandmother and running off so that her older "siblings" had to scour the neighborhood to find her. For years, I thought she was my mother's sister, truly my aunt. I must have been twelve-years-old when I discovered she was really my cousin! But, I know that even in these times, she was lonely. New restrictions placed on her by my disciplined grandmother took away from her the comfort of her friend, and soon to be nemesis – food.

As sisters often do, my mother and Aunt Pat shared child rearing duties. At eighteen, searching for something lost to her, alone again, and on her own, Aunt Pat took up residence at my Uncle Al's apartment; he was off traveling the world by this time as a Merchant Marine. Needless to say, it was at this time that my cousin, Akim, made his appearance.

Aunt Pat met my Uncle Teddy a few years later and my cousin, Tay, was born soon after. The story is similar to one that most families have. I gave him the nickname, Tay, because at age three, I could not pronounce *Theodore*. Aunt Pat and Uncle Teddy worked strange hours, and during the week Tay and Akim stayed with us. As our mothers before us, we also became siblings.

Memories about my Aunt Pat from this point in time revolve around two strange and compelling bedfellows – food and girdles. Ox tail soup, she insisted I eat. She made me sit at the table for hours. I refused to ingest the African American delicacy. When my father showed up to take my brother and I home, I was still sitting at the table. Although my Aunt Pat continued to insist I eat dinner before I go, my daddy picked me up and carried me out the door. I believe I stuck my tongue out at her over my father's shoulder as I departed!

I remember that she was always-buying girdles, trying on girdles, getting into girdles, and sitting around in girdles. When I was a teenager, we snuck and took pictures of her in her girdle! My Aunt Pat was a large woman. Daily occurrences from yesterday now play over sadly in my mind. I remember Aunt Pat eating huge quantities of food, drinking two-liter bottles of sodas by herself, not sharing her food, and being mad when we snuck some of her food. Uncle Teddy was the one who doled out the ice pops; Aunt Pat never offered.

Then, there was no name for the state that my beloved Aunt was in – today we call it Compulsive Overeating or Food Addiction – a very real and very dangerous disease. I believe that is what killed my Aunt Pat while she was thousands of miles away from me. Today, I admit that I suffer from, and struggle with, the same malady.

In January of 2007, I admitted my life had become unmanageable when I could not get out of my compact Toyota Corolla. To remove my girth, I had to turn sideways and scoot. At thirty-five-years-old, with hopes of still being a mother, I knew that my life had spun out of control.

I returned to a Twelve-Step program, an organization I had great success with in my twenties but had walked away from after becoming a Born Again Christian. I had been told that I was "delivered" from Food Addiction. I had Christ; I did not need Twelve Steps. Ignorant and ungodly advice, I followed. 100 pounds and ten years later found me stuck behind the wheel of my car. I did not want to die and so after much prayer and seeking of the Lord, I returned to the program.

There were not many African Americans there, but I found a great many Born Again Christians who shared with me that working the Twelve Steps was in line with Philippians 2 verse 12, *daily working out my salvation with fear and trembling.*

These Born Again Christians shared with me that others might make the group, the chair, or Buddha their higher power, but we knew the truth. We knew that there is only one God and only one mediator between God and man, the Savior Jesus Christ. I discovered that working a Twelve-Step program meant letting the light of God shine into all the dark corners of my life, daily submitting my will to God, and giving up the sin of idol worship – food was an idol and I was worshipping at the fridge daily.

I was almost 40 pounds lighter on the day I got the call about my Aunt Pat. But it was several days before I broke down, and when I did I was angry. I was not mourning, I was enraged. I remembered all the times when I was a teenager how my Aunt Pat encouraged me to explore my sexuality and how often I listened. What if she would have told me to remain pure for Christ, to turn to Him for every need? I was angry because as an adult, every time I spoke to her, she brushed off my attempts to share with her the love of Christ. Her mouth was so crass that I often rushed off the phone. I ignored her forwarded emails of irreverent jokes, mindless quotes, and silly stories, so caught up in her actions; I did not show her the love of Christ.

I was angry with myself, why hadn't I been more loving, why hadn't I taken the time to email back, why hadn't I showed her the love of Christ through my actions, and forgiven her? But most of all, I was angry that she had left me too soon, that she had never overcome the addiction that led her to the grave. But food is supposed to be so safe, and no one wants to admit that it can kill you, slow and steady, one bite at a time.

At the funeral I sang a song that I wrote and I didn't know how to respond when people said that my Aunt Pat was in a better place. How did they know? She never professed Christ to me; she never shared a salvation experience with my mother although my mother often witnessed to her.

How could I take comfort in their vain imaginings that my Aunt was somewhere on a beach or bellying up to the bar in heaven? I broke down. As my brother held me, I realized that I wasn't angry anymore. I reveled in the good things; the great memories came pouring back. Aunt Pat telling me that I was a great singer, us singing Motown together, practicing with our little singing groups at her house; we knew one day we'd be stars. I remembered fleeing to her house for comfort when I had a fight with my dad or when my mother just didn't understand, meeting her after work and browsing for hours at little Music Stores in the Village, walking to the movie theatre to see the latest Disney movie released from the Vault. My Aunt Pat loved me, she did the best she could by me, my regret is that I could have done better by her.

I thank the Lord that there is no condemnation to they who are in Christ Jesus and I rest in the Lord's mercy and pray my Aunt Pat received His grace – only the Lord knew her heart. Regardless, I am glad that one day when I am in His presence for eternity, I might look around and find that some of my loved ones are not there, but He will wipe every tear from my eye.

Food Addiction – it is a very real and very dangerous disease. And like all diseases, the Lord in His infinite wisdom may heal some from it with just a touch and others may have to have treatment. It is not about self-control. It is about the addictive qualities of sugar, of the "high" obtained from binging, and Food Addiction is a disease of the Spirit. It is the result of experiencing a life where you feel left out, alone, unloved. And not being pointed to the Author and Finisher of life itself, the very center of all that love is.

Every day, I must surrender my will to the Lord and allow Him to be everything to me, to realize that I don't have to turn to food because I am emotionally incapable of dealing with my life – everyday I practice doing all things through Christ who strengthens me, I deal with all the little foxes ruining my veins. I miss my Aunt Pat; I let too much time slip through my fingers. I let too many days go by without telling her I loved her. I let unspoken words keep me from sharing the love of Christ with her. When people don't know that Christ is everything, when they don't know that He is all they need, they look to other things to fill the void, alcohol, food, sex, drugs, they let their lives slip through their fingers and they don't even know it. I know, for I have already let valuable years of my own life slip through my fingers, losing days as I hid from the world and covered my pain with food instead of turning to the Lord.

But it won't happen again. I will not be quiet; I will not succumb to tradition and someone else's directive about how I should overcome the weight of the world that I have allowed to take up residence on my body. I will not be silent, I won't let another loved one slip through my fingers – and I will overcome by the blood of the lamb and the word of this testimony that I share with you. I remember my Aunt Pat and I can turn from the seductive calling of food and find the freedom I truly desire in the arms of the Lord. And, if I know anything about my Aunt, I know this - that is exactly what she would want me to do.

Dr. Naima Tonya Johnston is a Christian Recording Artist, Author, Educator, and Speaker. Traveling the country ministering in music and the word, Dr. Johnston is also the CEO of Broken Box Ministries, a Christian arts and education company dedicated to sharing the gospel of Christ in creative and unique ways. For more information contact Katapult Entertainment Group at 931-381-0032 or at naimasbrokenbox@yahoo.com. Visit Naima online at www.myspace.com/musicofnaima   www.shoutlife.com/Naima.

How I Found Helena

Helena Driscoll

I met him through mutual friends in late 1995, just six months after my first husband and I had separated. My first marriage had been difficult, with physical violence in the first few years which ended after one particularly bad beating. I stayed with my first husband on the firm understanding that if he ever laid another hand on me I would take our daughters and he would never see us again. To his credit, he never did lay another hand upon me. It lasted ten years until I realized I had nothing left to give to the relationship. We had met and married very young. We were two completely different people, traveling two completely different paths.

To say our split was amicable would be a lie. He was hurting and he lashed out. My life became filled with fear and worry as I was plagued by strange phone calls, stalking, nasty and disturbing letters in the mail, and incidences that left the local police tearing their hair out. Things were never resolved and it was at that time that I met the man that I thought I would spend the rest of my life with. He was everything my first husband had not been. He was caring, sweet, sensitive, attentive, and tender. Little did I to know that behind that façade lurked a monster.

Our relationship was fraught with difficulties and for the next ten years I discovered just how alone a person can be even when they are not.

Having come from a violent relationship previously, I was determined that no man would ever treat me that way again. When the "red flags" started to appear, I failed to recognize them. I was so unaware and naïve that when things started to happen I did not equate them with Domestic Violence. To me DV was a physical thing and even as aware as I was of the emotional and sometimes mental abuse that crept into our relationship, I still managed to convince myself that I wasn't a victim of DV. It didn't help that he was a consummate liar and arch manipulator; in fact, he was so good at it that for the second time, in this second relationship, I began to think that the problems lay within me.

My second marriage lasted ten years, as well. He would place a mild sleeping tablet into my drinks and take advantage of me while I was unconscious. I questioned him about it once but kept quiet after he told me that I appeared to be a more than willing participant. I often asked myself how I could possibly be a willing participant if I wasn't even aware of it happening.

After ten years, I started suffering severe insomnia and anxiety, constantly finding myself in tears. It was then that I decided that I needed some counseling. I will never forget the look of shock on my counselor's face when I told her what had been occurring. She was adamant that this was sexual abuse and it fell on deaf ears. Over the next few months, the "drink spiking" became a weekly, sometimes twice weekly, event. I issued him an ultimatum, giving him three months to make some changes or our marriage was over. Six weeks later and no attempt by him to exact any changes, I knew I was done. It was over - or so I would have liked to believe.

The next six months became a nightmare. He stalked me at every opportunity. He would show up wherever I was, attempted to befriend everyone that I associated with, made twice-daily visits to my home, and some nights came into my bedroom while I was sleeping. I turned to alcohol and drugs in an effort to become numb and hopefully in some way cope with what was happening.

One Friday night he was looking after the children while I went out. He made me a cup of tea when I returned. Half an hour later I knew I had again been drugged. I had let my guard down and he had taken advantage of that. I stumbled to my bed and passed out. Although heavily drugged, I was able to fight off his advances and screamed at him to leave my room. He had laced my tea with eight sleeping tablets.

The next morning, I was furious and told him in no uncertain terms to "get the hell out of my life." I went to my bedroom, locked the door, and proceeded to get changed. Within a couple of minutes he had unlocked the door, entered the room, closed and locked the door behind him, and calmly said "come here." I knew that I was in trouble, sensing that I was in extreme danger. His expressionless face was blank. I tried to scramble across the bed in an attempt to reach the door and hopefully escape. Within seconds, however, he was upon me, covering my nose and my mouth with his full weight, attempting to suffocate me.

I knew I was dying, that I would never be a part of this world again, and I started to black out. Two of my children were screaming and banging at the door. That was when I knew I could not say goodbye; I couldn't leave my children. One last effort to get a hand free proved successful and I managed to begin gauging at his eyes. This made him pull back enough that I was able to get my other hand free. I pulled at his hair, his ears, anything I could grab hold of.

He stopped, sat back, and told me to tell the children that everything was okay. I shook my head but with more menace in his voice he repeated his request. Too afraid of angering him further, I began crying as he undressed me. I begged him "no" as he raped me.

Afterwards, I lay there crying as he apologized and said, "I did it out of love."

I looked at him with disgust and said, "That's not love." He left the room. I lay there in the fetal position for some time before I arose, dressed, and then left the house.

I do not remember leaving. I actually don't remember much at all of the next three days. Somehow, I stayed upright through a blur of excruciating pain in my jaw which prevented me from opening my mouth to eat. There was more pain in my left shoulder where he had torn a tendon and damaged the ligaments and surrounding muscles.

On the following Tuesday, I snapped out of the shock enough to realize that I was still in danger and decided that I would take out an Apprehended Violence Order. I found myself giving robotic statements as I suffered through a "Sexual Assault Examination" with calmness that I did not feel inside of me. It was not until I was asked the question, "Is he a good father?" and "Good fathers don't rape the mothers of their children, especially with them there, do they?" that I realized I wanted him charged.

The next 18 months was a Ferris wheel of emotions, wondering how I got through the rough time. The thing that stuck in my head was what gave me the determination to see my husband face up to what he had done to me. I had never felt so betrayed. He had taken something from me, and I wanted it back. When people asked, "Why are you letting them charge him?" The answer always remained the same. "For my children, because they have to grow up understanding the difference between right and wrong, and that there are consequences for doing the wrong thing. Even Daddies have to take responsibility for their actions," I'd tell them.

I wasn't the first one that this had happened to, and I wouldn't be the last. I wanted to make certain that he would not hurt another woman. One day another woman would fall for his charms. Another woman would suffer, only the next one might not be so lucky to escape with her life. I couldn't allow that to happen, no matter what.

The court process was long and frustrating which was made even more difficult by his release from prison on bail. He didn't waste any time smooth-talking his way back into our lives. I allowed him to a certain degree. In hindsight, it was a foolish thing to do but he still had the power to manipulate me and he knew just how to do it. I applied to the Family Court for a divorce and the Magistrate was only too happy to grant it. I was no longer his wife.

Let the Healing Begin

I moved back to Queensland to live with my daughters who were now eighteen and twenty years of age. I began studying, doing my Diploma in Justice Administration with the idea of one day becoming a Domestic Violence Court Support Worker. I passed top of my class with Distinctions and Credits and I began to feel that I was once again a worthwhile and intelligent woman.

There were many days when I fell apart as I didn't talk about what had happened to anyone, instead choosing to bottle everything up. I rarely allowed my feelings to show and I often got through my days by clenching my teeth and pushing everyone away. After seven months or so, I decided I needed to move back to NSW. I needed to face my demons head on and get on with my life.

During this time, I began spending a lot of time on the Internet. I slowly began forming strong friendships with people; many of whom had been through Domestic Violence. Suddenly I did not feel so alone and I learned to reach out. More importantly, I learned to open up. It was, and still is, those friendships that helped me to face each day, to carry on, to continue fighting. I felt like I was doing it for us all.

I had been suffering nightmares. These had somewhat dissipated, too, and I began to look forward to each day with renewed enthusiasm.

It finally came to the trial. An hour before the trial was to begin, I was called into an office and informed that he had changed his plea to guilty with the condition of having one of the lesser charges dropped. At first, I adamantly refused until it was made clear to me that getting a conviction of rape in a small country town was nearly impossible. I eventually agreed. He was formally charged and convicted on one count of "Sexual Assault without Consent." There were a couple of charges of "Sexual Assault" as well as "Attempted Sexual Assault." It would take another four months before he was sentenced.

In the meantime, I found myself in a much happier state of mind and I discovered that support comes in many different ways. I started to believe that I would indeed come out of this a much better and a much stronger person. I began writing as I found that I could finally express my innermost thoughts which brought along with it the realization that I had so many people pulling for me every step of the way. They believed in me and this in turn gave me the ability to finally believe in myself.

On December 3, 2007, my ex-husband was sentenced to five years imprisonment with a non-parole period of 2 ½ years. The Judge who handed down the sentence simply stated that he "believed me." The Judge continued saying that my ex-husband is an "extremely selfish man who reacts violently when he doesn't get what he wants." He expressed his disgust at a man who would rape his own wife, regardless of the fact they were separated, and even more disgust at his doing this with the children present.

I sat there with tears silently running down my face. I had been vindicated.

My sister, the only person throughout this whole ordeal who had shown me unwavering belief and support, held my hand tightly. We had won.

I felt like I had gotten my life back that day; that I'd been set free. Since sentencing I have had my ups and downs, especially when I realize what I face. The realization that I am now raising three boys on my own, the youngest of whom is disabled, is sometimes overwhelming. Some days have been exceptionally hard, especially when I still have to deal with his friends who treat me like a pariah for sending the "poor guy" to prison and separating him from his children.

I stand up for myself, I don't back down and I do this with pride, for myself and for my children. No matter what, I did the right thing and nobody can ever take that away from me. Some days are exceptionally hard. I struggle financially and every so often I wonder just how I am going to be able to manage. Some days I cannot cope, I do not want to cope, I get tired of coping - of being a machine. Those are the days when I stop and take a breath, where I allow myself to be human, to feel, even if it is painful. Those are the days where I embrace every emotion and recognize that these emotions are mine.

Those are the days that allow me to get back up and keep going.

Helena Driscoll lives in Australia with her sons. She is an advocate against Domestic Violence.

That Night with Julie

Robin Rice

"You're Robin Rice?" the young, dark-haired woman asked me.

We were in line, signing in for an open mike poetry reading at the local bookstore. I'm not exactly a household name, but as I am an author, some people know of my work. Despite my own "off" mood, which had been in a downward spiral for weeks, I was prepared to put on a polite smile. One look into this young woman's deeply troubled face and I knew this was not the tack to take. You don't have to be a psychic to know what that kind of face means. You only have to have been there yourself. This woman-child was on the edge of her own life, and looming toward a jump.

"Yes," I answered.

"I hear you know something about depression," she said, looking at me with both need and suspicion. Her name was Julie, and, as it turned out, her mother knew someone who knew someone else who had been depressed and come to me for spiritual healing. I've always been willing to share my story about overcoming 25 years of recurring depression, but this night I didn't have much to give. It was tempting to hand her my card, tell her to give me a call.

Something inside said, Talk to her. Now. Tomorrow may not come.

We both had our hot drinks, and our names were well down the list for performing our poems. We agreed to move to two comfy chairs and relative solitude. An eerie feeling came over me, as if everyone else in the store had disappeared. It was just me, Julie, and a lot of books.

Visions of my little brother, Ricky, flashed in front of my eyes. He had been where Julie was when he was eighteen-years-old. I hadn't lived close enough to see the desperation in his eyes, and it was still hard to admit I had not heard it in his voice on the phone only days before his suicide.

My body trembled. Something in this encounter was beginning to feel like a possible redemption. Even though my life was already devoted to helping others, this felt different. This was youth in its prime and beauty, yet with no vision, no sense of the value in living, no future to walk towards. I did not know how to address such a travesty. I could only hope my best would be enough.

"You must be willing to recover your soul," I said.

She looked at me blankly. I decided to start again. "If you want to live a soulful life, which is the only way I know to truly relieve depression, you must be willing to be who you really are - to look at the world through different eyes than the ones you've been trained to use your whole life. You must be willing to drop to a deeper level of existence, a level that is pleading to you through the worst of your days, asking you to listen to it. You must be willing to look for the legend that is trying to be told within your own life." I took another deep breath, surprised at the lofty nature of my own words, but unwilling to tone them down. Something was unraveling in me. It was going to have its say.

"To live a soulful life, you must be willing to not fit in. Because if you are this deeply hurt by life at this young an age, you don't fit in. You never will, at least not in the usual ways. I'm sorry if that disappoints you, but we might as well be honest. What the surface level of life is selling you will never satisfy your kind. But that's okay. It's never satisfied a lot of the most amazing people that have ever lived."

Julie pulled a small notebook out of her purse and began writing. It encouraged me to go on.

"To live a soulful life, you must be willing to stand alone, up against what everyone and everything in our society tells you is right for you, and ask what your heart wants, what your very being desires. You have to be willing to love who you really love, not who you are supposed to love."

I shifted toward her, lowering my voice to deliver the greatest of secrets. "Let me tell you something. When people come to see me, I ask them who and what really turns them on, what calls them to their depths. Most often, they say they don't know. But I don't buy it. They do know. It is just that their answers are not on the "good for you" or "easily attainable" list. Or, they don't know how to get what they truly love without losing something else they think is their life depends on. So they've shoved what they love into a closet and often forgotten it entirely.

"These loves are really callings. They are the are pearls of great price we must travel to the ends of the earth for. But very few among us talk about that heroic journey anymore, so very few actually embark on one. If you want a soulful life, you must be willing to listen for that call, and follow it whatever the cost."

I saw a light sparkle in Julie's eye. I could see her rummaging through her memories, then finding something of worth. I didn't need to know what she found. I trusted it, whatever it was.

"To live a soulful life, you must be willing to encounter obstacles. We live in an age where people think that the smooth road is a sign they are on the right road-that if God has called you to something, but barriers arise, then either you have been abandoned or you must have gotten the call wrong in the first place. It's not so. These very barriers are also the hand of God, preparing you to receive the bounty. You would not be wise enough to keep what you find otherwise. It's worked this way throughout history and in every corner of the world. Every modern invention we have will not change those rules. Just ask Joseph Campbell, one of my closest personal friends."

"I thought he was dead," Julie remarked, surprising me that she knew of him at all.

"His body is," I admitted. "But his soul lives on, here in this bookstore and countless personal and public libraries across the world. To live a soulful life, you must be willing to make friends with your kind of people in whatever way you can."

"I never meet my kind of people," she said, her eyes flashing with both profound sadness and fresh-cut anger.

"That's my point. I don't meet them very often either. But they can be found here," I said, pointing toward the vast array of books along the shelves. "David Whyte is one of my greatest soul supports, though I've never met him. Annie Dillard, too. And, Arnie Mindell and Thomas Moore and Rilke and Kipling and Krishnamurti. I tell you, Lao-Tzu and all his translators often keep me company late at night, when the 3 AM witching hour strikes me dead awake in an empty house. I don't have to have tea with them to feel their presence, to not feel so alone. They are my people. Time and space matter little to the soul."

Julie sighed. I knew she wanted better than that. I often do, too. But life is what it is. Real hands to hold are not always available.

"And speaking of that 3 AM witching hour," I continued, "to live a soulful life, you must be willing to make it your friend. I always say, nobody soul searches on a good day. And the night terrors that come and magnify your every fear visit for a reason. Don't push them away. Listen to them. They can tell you things about your deepest self you won't hear in the daytime." Julie kept writing, her hand moving as fast as I've seen a hand move over the page. If anyone else was listening, I didn't know and didn't care. Something was speaking from my depths, and I was not about to stop it from coming through. Whether it was helping my young friend or not, I needed to hear what I was saying.

"To live a soulful life, you must be willing to look at your choices carefully. To notice when you choose too much, or not enough. When you want to go left, but you go right. When you want to act but don't, or don't want to act but do. You must see when you sabotage your own soul's longings, and when you indulge to the point it harms you. You must look squarely at your addictions and notice what happens when they are denied. If you can do this, just look clearly and honestly - what the Masters would call Becoming The Witness - you won't have to do much more. Like turning your car in the direction of a skid, the looking itself initiates the balance that is being sought.

"To live a soulful life, you must be willing to pull yourself away from the herd that is our mass culture, to turn off the messages thrown at you both in television shows and in the commercials between them. Their mandate is to tell you who you are, and who you want to be, and how to get there... which of course is to buy something that can never bring you to a soulful existence. They want you to be a consumer, and consumers don't have souls."

Julie shifted in her seat. I could see the idea of turning of the TV was a little too much for my young companion.

"Remember, I'm suggesting you must be willing to follow these suggestions. When you are depressed, actually following them may be beyond your capacity. But being willing, it can happen of its own accord, in time. With willingness, the gods have a road on which to move you. You might have to wait a while, but by simply being willing, or even by being willing to become willing, the journey is begun."

For what seemed an endless time, I mused aloud with Julie taking notes. I spoke of strength and virtue, alienation and death, beauty and longing. I spoke of offering the imperfect offering, how nature models the way for us, and how the wars of the world speak to the wars within. Whenever I needed a quote from one of my close personal friends, I found the very book waiting on a shelf and a uncannily keen memory of what words were where. A great stack of books grew. I secretly hoped Julie would take home one or two - something to hold her through the night.

Finally, and all of a sudden, I was spent. I had said all I knew to say. As if on cue, my name was called from a distance. The bookstore slammed back into reality. I moved to the mike to read the only poem of my own that my spent brain could remember:

Big Weaving

You cannot keep to plans that are big.

You can only keep to plans that are small

Staying very focused, very certain

Very sure you are being honorable

To your word.

To live a big life you can only go

Where the way opens like a weaver

Not knowing what she weaves

Tying knots when the thread runs out wherever that may be,

And starting again

With whatever new thread is at hand.

From this side of a future

With no plans

It seems impossible

You are weaving anything of value at all.

Yet all of the big weavers,

The true artists will tell you this:

On the other side of your days you will see

The other side of your tapestry.

Looking back,

All that was random will reveal itself

As supremely inspired, orchestrated

From a greater place, a stronger hand

Than your smaller, planning self

Could have imagined

Let alone dared.

From this vantage point your heart

Will swell and your eyes

Will tear and your center

Will grow strong so that you feel yourself

Planted as solid as a many-seasoned tree.

In this other-side gaze you will finally know

With utter certainty that Divinity was as big

As you allowed It to be.

When I looked up, I saw Julie at the door, offering a small smile and an abbreviated wave. Beyond her, where we were sitting, I saw she'd left every book I suggested, and even her own notebook. The host of the open mike called her name next, speaking it again and again. With each, "Julie? Julie?" I felt a crushing sense of failure, as if Ricky had come to give me another chance, and I'd blown it.

That is, until I leafed through Julie's notebook. Inside was everything I'd said written in beautiful, gentle hand writing. The only words she offered of her own were these: "Robin, share with others."

To this day, I don't know what happened to Julie. I don't know if she lived or died or something in between. But I myself was lifted that night, and pointed again in the direction of my own soul's recovery. So much so, I've at times wondered if Julie was a desperate young girl at all, or Something More appearing- as Something More so often does- in disguise.

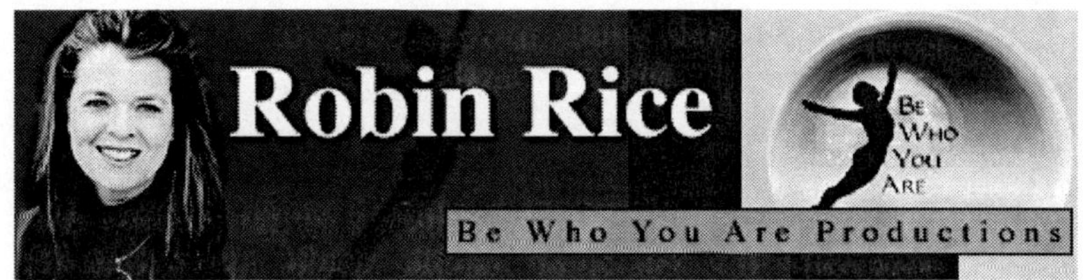

Robin Rice is an Author, Spiritual Mentor, and contemporary Shaman. Visit her on the web at www.BeWhoYouAre.com

NOTE: This article first appeared in Natural Beauty and Health Magazine.

No Such Thing as Rock Bottom
Nkechi Feaster

I have always been afraid of heights. I would believe that anyone else with this particular phobia would agree that it's not the idea of being that high up from the ground that makes it scary, but rather the idea of falling from that high up. The falling stirs the actual fear. The idea of falling is what actually scares me to death. I've spent a large portion of my life falling but I have never hit rock bottom. The only time that there even is a rock bottom is in the case of a physical fall. At some point a fall will result in hitting something. But in the many different situations that life brings you, there is no bottom.

It seems as though I have spent the majority of my twenty-three years of existence falling. For over two decades, I'd continually been pushed and thrown from cloud nine, never once hitting the ground. As a result, I'd spent plenty of times committing mental and emotional suicide by jumping from grace. I hit many blocks on my way down each time I fell, but I never hit rock bottom. I just kept falling.

"Why me?" was the only question I had ever brought to God. In October of 2001, I stood asking myself that question again. It would be the last time.

At that moment, everything I owned was packed into four bags. I had my son, who was six- or seven- years-old at that time. I was feeling angry, hurt, scared, and betrayed again and more like a failure than I had ever felt in my life. I couldn't believe that I was being kicked out of yet another person's house. Everyone that I'd ever stayed with had put me out. Most of the time, it was without time to find somewhere else to go. Two of those times, I was pregnant. I had run out of people to live with. There was no one else I knew that would or could allow me and my son to stay under his or her roof.

I had burned many bridges, and still wasn't yet ready to take responsibility for my part in what transpired between me and those that I had burned bridges with. My son and I were waiting for a ride to pick us up from a friend's house where we'd been staying in Maryland to go to a shelter in Washington, D.C. and I was terrified. I had no idea what to expect from this place, but was grateful that they even had room for us. I certainly did not want to end up on the streets. If they hadn't accepted us, the street is most certainly where we would have ended up.

As I waited, I began to think of how I had gotten to this point. I had been through many things in my life that I'd never dealt with; molestation and being gang-raped before I turned fifteen. As a result, I ended up doing what many young women who suffered through the same painful circumstances ended up doing - I slept around. The whole *looking for love in the wrong places* concept was one that I'd lived by for a very long time. I was carrying around a lot of guilt because I felt that my promiscuity is what led to my rape. Even with that load of guilt, I still never stopped having sex. By the time I got to college, I was no longer under my mother's loving, yet watchful eye, and I went crazy with it.

Just about every time I lay down with someone, I got up with much less; less inner peace and less happiness. Less contentment with not being the person I wanted to be and could not for the life of me seem to get to. There are things I got up with more of, such as more guilt, more self-loathing, and more self-hatred. That is one hard pill to swallow. It wasn't my fault that I'd suffered the traumas that I suffered. I didn't know how to stop the acts that I was doing as a result of others. So, further I fell.

At some point, I began to start liking myself, although only on the most miniscule of levels. I began to feel that I wasn't as bad as I'd let the actions of others all my life lead me to believe. I have a big heart. I am smart; very smart. I even began to feel attractive, which I had never dared think before. I got along with many different types of personalities who all seemed to genuinely like me for me. That was promising. It was also such a shock to my system that it made my mind hurt. I began to feel idiotic for taking the opinions of others as my opinion of myself.

Unfortunately, because I would never take the time to deal with anything else that I'd been through, this wasn't really good for me. I did not stop pushing myself from grace. But, not for trying; I was actually able to get into a relationship. To this date, it is one of the best relationships I'd ever been in. I was never in love with him, but I don't think he'll ever know how good to and for me he was. He felt I was attractive, but was one of the first to not treat me as just someone to lay down with. He felt that I was intelligent enough to actually have conversation with. We spent a lot of time together; we grocery shopped and cooked together. We would spend days in the house listening to music and cuddled up while each of us read our own book. My son would be running around as little children do. It was an ideal situation.

Because of that situation, I began to filter my mind with not only the things that he saw in me, but what I saw in myself. My confidence, for the first time in my life, started to poke its head from under the covers that it had been hiding under for all of my life. I wasn't yet ready to deal with my past traumas, but I was ready to stop the self-loathing. I wish it could have lasted longer.

I am not sure why or how, but the relationship changed. It became monotonous, and not in a way that was comfortable. We had somehow gone from one of us cooking a fabulous dinner, either watching television, listening to music or just having great conversations, followed by having consensually great intimate moments to him coming over, eating, watching television alone, having sex with me, and then going to sleep.

I didn't know if it was something that I had done to make his actions towards me change, but I could no longer take his actions. I was left feeling the same way as I had felt after being with any other man before him. After beginning to fill my inner-self with positivity, I was not ready to go back to feeling that type of negatively.

So, I told him that I needed a break. In hindsight, I should have sat him down and talked to him about how I was feeling so that we could have attempted to work it out. But that is not what I did. I just asked him to leave so that I wouldn't feel the negative emotions that he was leading me to feel. Unfortunately, God had other plans. The events that followed were many hard lessons that I had to learn. Although, I would fall much further before I actually learned them.

At that time I was working at one of the colleges in Raleigh, NC in the shipping and receiving department. I was doing well there, too. I'd made friends and that job was one of the things in my life that was showing me that I wasn't such a bad person as I had led myself to believe. The people that I worked with probably didn't know how I felt about myself. I was rather boastful. It was not a cover-up. After all, I was still in the process of filtering the positive into my psyche and soul. I was the person that I was portraying myself to be. It was just the first time in my life I was acting as I wanted to act. I was becoming more outgoing and less afraid of the world and the people in it. I liked the person I was. I wish that could have lasted longer. But, again, God had a plan for my life.

It was during the summer and after my 23rd birthday. One of my best friends and I had spent a weekend in Maryland with another best friend to celebrate the event. These were, at the time, two of the closest people in my life so it was also one of the best weekends . . . and much needed. Afterwards, my life made a turn. I made one of the biggest mistakes I would ever make.

The campus was empty during the summer and was going through revitalization. There was construction going on in many of the dorms and other buildings on campus. There were workers all over the place, as well. I met one of them. He started saying hello to me every time he saw me, more than once a day. Raised with good manners, I was cordial. No other response is necessary if he doesn't say hello, and I later wished that he greeted me with something more along the lines of, *Hey, Shorty, Damn, girl!*, or something similar. That way, I could have ignored him and the events that followed never would have happened.

Instead, he was always cordial. Again, that left me obligated to be cordial. When he said hello, I said hello. When he asked how I was doing, I answered. When he asked to take me out for lunch, I allowed it.

I was in no way, shape, fashion, or form attracted to this older man. He was not a handsome man in the least. He was too skinny. I was not attracted to him; I was actually repulsed by the sight of him. One lesson that I learned later was to tell a man that I am not interested if I was not. I did not do that with him. I humored him. I finally gave in after he repeatedly asked me to go out with him; my first and only pity date, to date.

I agreed to join him for a movie. He arrived at my house around five forty-five that evening. The movie didn't start until seven o'clock. In my mind, I heard bells and whistles going off. That seemed a little too eager for my level of comfort, but I continued to humor him. I let him in. We sat and talked, he on one end of my couch while I sat on the other end. I didn't want to get too close. I only wanted to go to the movies and never have to deal with him again.

As the time for us to leave approached, he made no move to leave. He only made moves on me. As subtle as they were, they made me even more uncomfortable. I didn't want him to touch my arm, shoulder, hand, or any other part of my person. Every time he tried to, I would move his hand and ask him not to do that. He had slyly ended up sitting right beside me on the couch after continually getting up and pacing around the living room and sitting back down. Each time he sat down, he would move closer to me.

I have lied about the events that followed for years. At that time, I was very confused. Regardless of the fact that I was starting to gain some self-love, I still had a lot of things inside that I had yet to deal with. I still had not come to terms with what I'd been through, be it by the hands of others or by my own actions. I still had a lot of guilt that I hadn't gotten rid of. I could not do anything about being molested and gang-raped, but I could have chosen not to sleep around as much as I had. Because of the insecurities that I still felt, I continued to seek acceptance. I wanted to feel desired, loved, appreciated. During that time, although it was starting to diminish, I still slept with most of the men I slept with simply because they showed an interest in me. That's all it took; *looking for love in all the wrong places.* So, when this man that I was so not attracted to that he repulsed me continued whispering sweet nothings in my ears, I took it as acceptance and chose to allow him to seduce me. I willingly lay down with a man who I knew I didn't want to be with just because he said he liked me. I would not realize this until long after these events transpired and after I suffered from the tremendous guilt of what happened next.

Guilt still plagues me from the events of that night because after choosing to sleep with this man, he raped me. How is that possible, you ask? Well, while we were having relations, he asked if he could have anal sex with me. Since the very thought of such an act turned me off to the point that I could lose my drive, I said no. This was something that I would never try. I had absolutely no desire to take part in such an act that disgusted me. He did it anyway. I was held down and forced against my will, all the while saying no. Crying and pleading made no difference to him. It was the most horrific thing I have yet to encounter. Afterwards, when I tried to make him leave, he said that I couldn't say anything because I was a willing participant, which I couldn't deny. So, would it still be considered rape? If I was to file charges and we ended up in court, every sexual act that I had participated in would have been brought out. I could not deal with that. I was not strong enough. He knew that and used it against me.

Even with those facts, I didn't want to see him. I did not want to look into his face. I wasn't attracted to him, but I agreed to sleep with him. I agreed to sleep with him and he took full advantage of that, but I didn't feel that there was anything that I could ever do about it but live with it. I didn't have to live with him, so I told him to leave. He then told me that he was in the mob and that if I put him out or told anyone about what had transpired, he would have my entire family killed, forcing me to watch. He wouldn't have me killed after that, because he wanted to be with me. He wanted to marry me. I didn't want to be with or around this man and the very thought of it made me ill. When he went to work, I went to a friend's house; a friend that I had been physically involved with and very attracted to when I was in college.

I asked him to buy some marijuana. I wanted to escape from my mind and the terrible things running through it. He obliged and we sat and got high together. We did not have sex, but it was tempting. When I went home, my rapist had returned and was waiting for me. He swore that I had cheated on him and beat me for an act that I had never engaged in.

This was my nightmare. He moved in the next day. From that point on, I had to convince a man who raped me that I loved him while he beat me for the smallest indiscretion because if I did not he'd have my whole family killed. Of course, there was nothing I felt that I could do but to take it. One month after he moved in he asked me if I had ever done any drug besides marijuana. I told him no. He said that crack wasn't that bad and that I might like it. I was afraid to actually say no, but knew that as long as he was around, I would not smoke with him. I was certain that he would lace anything that he gave me. That didn't stop him from smoking crack, however.

Growing up in an extremely small town and having a very protective mother kept me from experiencing a lot of things, good and bad. I'd never seen anyone high on drugs before. I couldn't tell you how someone high on dippers, crack, cocaine or any other drug acted or what they looked like while they were intoxicated. That's why I didn't know that my rapist was a crack-head. The drug was his only means of covering the insecurities that resided in him. The insecurities he felt for himself were massive, I knew that. I knew that was why I was beaten.

Abusers have no idea that what they don't feel for themselves can never be replaced by anyone else if it's not within them to begin with. That's why I always fell short in his eyes, regardless of what I did. It's why he presented himself to others to be much more than the person he actually was.

The drugs were much needed and costly. He made me stop working and remove my son from daycare, which meant that he, being the only one in the house who worked, was responsible for paying all of the bills. Well, drug addicts don't pay bills. Every cent went to his drug of choice. I came to despise him and the drug itself. From that day on, for a very long time, I would despise anyone who partook of crack or any form of it because it reminded me of him.

For the next four months, this was my life. Trying to simply stay alive while continually being beaten and threatened for nothing. I'm an outgoing and very talkative person, but around him I was extremely meek and quiet. There was nothing I could do or say that would ever satisfy him, so I stayed as quiet as possible. It didn't stop him from abusing me; physically and verbally. He beat me when he could not perform adequately, never admitting that it was the drugs in his system that inhibited his performance.

Four months is not nearly as long as many others have suffered in similar circumstances, but four months in hell is more than long enough when it is your hell.

From August to December of 1998, I was in hell. I couldn't tell my family everything that went on because they would not have believed me anyway. I felt that I had put them through much, and they knew my track record of being irresponsible and promiscuous. Maybe they thought that it was a shame that I had gotten myself into my current situation, but it was my own fault. I have yet to tell a family member what happened during those four months because I believed that they would feel that I was making excuses in one way or the other, as I'd done so many times before when I needed help out of my own messes. My family had become used to me foolishly spending my money and then turning to them to pay whatever bills needed to be paid. Why should they be so willing to help me now? I had burned too many bridges with too many of them; even my mother.

During the time I spent with my captor, he talked a lot about his life. I learned that he was lying about much of it. One night as we sat at the kitchen table, I asked him how he met his son's mother. Listening to him, I realized that there was no way the story he told could have possibly been true. He started his story in one city at one time describing things that transpired that led him to another city during another time. In telling his story, describing events, times and places, he probably went through about five or six different cities, all of which were supposed to lead him to the time, place, and events where he met his son's mother. So, I wondered when he finished, how was it that his story led him through all of that but he ended up exactly in the city and time that he was in when he started telling me his story over two hours before?

When he finished his story and it was obvious to me that he was telling a huge lie, I said nothing. He was lying and had been the entire time I had been with him. How much had he lied about? Had he lied about being involved in the mob? Were the threats to murder my entire family just that? Were these threats only meant to keep a naïve woman under his thumb? There was only one way I would find out.

The next day he returned from work and I told him to give back my house key and to leave. He could not for the life of him figure out what had changed. No one shot me as soon as the words left my mouth, as he had me to believe would happen. No one kidnapped me or even approached me.

I was glad that my prayers to God were being answered, but I felt like the biggest idiot in the world. The guilt piled onto my shoulders and soul, too. I couldn't handle it. I especially couldn't handle the fact that all I'd wanted to do was forget that the last four months had ever happened, but he wouldn't leave me alone. He tried desperately to get me to take him back, resorting even to such means as contacting every person that I'd ever introduced him to and asking them to talk to me. I was screaming in my head and heart. Why wouldn't he just go away? Why couldn't he just leave me alone?

There's No Such Thing as Rock Bottom

I was emotionally, physically, mentally, and spiritually drained. I had nothing left but guilt and anger. I knew it was time for me to leave when I left my house with the intent to take a man's life. I have a good friend to thank for that not happening. I am a very loving person, who reached a point that I could not deal with. I was determined to make him leave me alone.

When I was unsuccessful, I was left with an emptiness that I had never felt in my life. I called one of my best friends who lived in Maryland and said, "I'm tired." I didn't yell it or even say it with anger. I imagine I just sounded as exhausted as I felt. She then told her boss that she was leaving to come to North Carolina to get her friend and that they would discuss whether or not she still had a job on Monday when she returned. And she came to get me. Yes, she is the epitome of a best friend, to this day.

I'd been falling in my life for as long as I could remember, never once hitting anything but despair on my way down. Not every time I fell was by my own actions, but there was no way I could escape that the past four months were my fault. I'd lost my apartment, watched my son change before my eyes, without him ever even being touched by my captor, and I lost every bit of the little love I had for myself. After moving to Maryland, I continued to fall.

As I said in the beginning, I was put out of every person's house that I'd ever lived with; friends, family, my father. None of them had a choice after the things I had brought to their homes. I was still being promiscuous, all the while feeling nothing but guilt and anger. I continually pushed myself from grace and fell further and further for another three years. I had yet to hit rock bottom. And I never would.

Making Positive Changes

Having to take my son and go into a shelter in October of 2000 was one of the most terrifying experiences I have yet to encounter in my life. After getting there and realizing just how tired I was of my life, I decided to change it. I knew that it would take more than securing a school for my son and making sure that he had somewhere to lay his head at night. I knew that it would take more than acquiring some type of schooling or training so that I could get a job that would pay enough for me to properly be a single mother. I knew that I had to change me. I also knew that I could not do this on my own. So I started therapy.

I think I talked for a year straight before my therapist and I even got to a point of trying to figure out how to deal with everything that was inside of me. Before that time, I didn't even know that there was that much bothering me. No wonder I was so promiscuous. No wonder I could not hold down a job. No wonder my son was so angry with me at the age of only six. No wonder I continued to fall for so much of my life. Well, still never yet hitting rock bottom, I began to climb up.

I gained stability for my son and me. I have been able to sustain employment, regained the love and trust of my son, love and trust for myself, and found happiness, and peace. Factors that I never had before, I am now determined to keep in my life. Being happy and at peace is the first thing to me. I have been through so much in my life and, now, I have dealt with it all. Some things still linger, like the guilt from my past actions, but nothing that remains is, nor will ever be, enough to hold me back again. I will never participate in the things that I put myself through in the past. Even if I should happen to come across another person who violates me, it will not strip me nearly as much as it has. I will heal because I can heal, because I have healed.

There is nothing that I cannot get through. Nothing life brings me will ever leave me in the state I was in. I know my faith also has a very large part to do with the person I am now. I have no regrets. Everything that I've been through, exactly as I went through it, is what has led me to be the person that I am now.

I love the woman God has shaped me into and is further shaping me into. My sense of peace has never been so massive.

I tell my story all the time because I know how it feels and I want to see everyone who has ever suffered anything even remotely similar to what I have been through get through it. I want to see everyone healed. I have always had enough love to help heal the world, now I have enough wisdom to help, as well.

It is, I believe, part of God's plan for my life. I now know that although there is no such thing as rock bottom, there is such a thing as climbing to the top.

 **Nkechi Feaster** resides in the Washington, D.C. area with her son. To contact Nkechi please email her at *innapeace@yahoo.com*

Learning How to Deal with the Weather

Eva Angvert Harren

It was the first day at the therapist's office. I knew on one level, that I should be there, but it felt strange. When I told Mom that I had received eight sessions from the insurance company and only had to pay a small co-pay, her response was, *"Isn't there anybody else who needs it more?"* That felt strange, too. It was often about others who needed it more; others who were more important.

My therapist, Dory, was a specialist who had a Ph.D. in Psychology and specialized in women who had lost children. After Kristina died, I became a mother with a dead child. I was thirty-two-years-old in 1990. I had sobered up that January. Lying in bed throwing up, thinking, *if this is how it is to be sober, I'll get drunk!* Little did I know that I was pregnant.

Kristina was born September thirtieth that year. I had never had a feeling like the one I had for Kristina. I held her and I could feel a warm soothing wave come through me like the first couple of drinks; my body would calm down, the shaking and itching would stop. Left was this wonderful sensation of a smooth warm secure blanket. The same feeling I get when I hug my family today; magical, always magical. I was ten months sober when Kristina arrived. Before that year, I don't remember too many days of not being drunk or thinking about drinking. Kristina truly replaced the alcohol... for a while.

In 1971, I had my first drink when I was thirteen and a half. The rest is a blur of confusion, drama, and pain. A lot of pain, it seems like. Maybe I did need therapy. That day at my first session, I was pregnant again. After the Ob/Gyn exam, the nutritionist told me to find a therapist. *Why? I don't need therapy.* This wonderful person looked straight into my eyes and said, "You lost your child! You are pregnant again. You're too stressed, too tense. Too crazy! You're hurting your baby. If you cannot do it for you, do it for the baby!"

I didn't know how to do things for myself, but I had learned very early how to do things for others; men in particular...

Kristina had died the same year she was born, December 1, 1990 at sixty-one-days old, or young. She did not just die. She had a heart operation. A heart operation on an infant! Her heart was no bigger than the top of my thumb. I know because I saw it! The nurse asked if we wanted to see her heart. We thought she was joking. "I am changing the dressing, do you want to watch?" Well, it was all a nightmare anyway, why not.

She removed the patch of 'pig skin' over the hole in Kristina's chest and said there is her heart, like; there is her toe, with no difference in her voice! I looked, my brain went blank, and a chill came over me. This was insanity. We were not supposed to see our child's heart... literally. That night I made a deal with God, *Hey God, if you exist, then you let her live, and I'll believe... anything!* Don't make deals with God! After two days in ICU there was no hope of her ever waking up again. So, if you love them, you let them go, don't you?

You make the decision to turn off the life support because your child is not really alive. I stood over her that Friday; she was pink, with fourteen needles in her body, a 'pig skin' that covered the hole in her chest. I felt a 'puff of air' and a weird sensation up my left eye. I looked back at Kristina. She was gray... she was gone... I knew it, I saw it. If we have a soul, hers just left. I called Bob, "She's gone!" The rest was just procedures. If it was not for technology she would have been gone sooner, but now the ICU got to charge for two more days.

They still said *'maybe'*. That is a weird word, *maybe*. All the doctors have to say is *maybe*, and we are willing to do anything: mortgage the house, spend our savings, borrow money, and put ourselves at risk for the rest of our lives. Just for another day with our dying child. Doctors should not be allowed to say *maybe*.

So, we turned her off! It was the longest three minutes of my life. They closed the curtains. "It's too messy," they said. After seeing her heart, how could anything be too *messy*? Why couldn't I have been allowed to hold her hand when they turned her off? Not even a flicker of compassion. Then we waited... for Kristina to die. You wait, and wait for that dang machine to stop beeping. Silence; so silent. It all stopped. *Wait a minute, are you sure she's not getting better? I'm sorry, I wasn't thinking right...*

The nurse came out behind the curtain and handed us a little bundle of towels... cold towels, and said, "Do you want to say goodbye?"

What? *Do you want to say goodbye?* Have these people totally lost any sense of decency *Oh, is that... Kristina? I'm sorry, that doesn't look like her. She is too... gray... too stiff... too dead. Is that Kristina? Did I even have a baby? My body feels like I did. Is this just a mean dream? Have I been drinking? Goodbye, Kristina. I love you, I mean, I loved you. No, wait, I still love you... so much...it hurts so much. I know.*

This one is a big one... too big, even for the booze to take away. The booze took away a lot, helped me endure life. Not that I was particularly fond of living. I just did!

It felt strange. It was just two months after she was in my belly. It was not supposed to go like this. There was a hole there, a bottomless hole, room for every bottle in the universe! I had never felt that kind of pain! Everything I had been through didn't even leave a dent in this one. My breasts still had milk, for God sake! But no one to feed... how does that work? "Just wait," the nurse said. "They will wean themselves." She said it as if the breasts had a life of 'their own'.

My body did have a life of its own. It itched, shook, got hot, then cold. The shaking was irritating and took a lot of attention, like standing on an earthquake. How do you have a relationship with anybody if all you can think of is not to fall over? What really pushed me over the edge were the unbearable aches in my gut and those pressures in my chest. I would explode, with no reason; the pressure would go down... and then... start building again. I knew a couple of drinks would calm it all down, but just for a moment. Then I would have to 'chase that dragon' again. I had chased it for almost 20 years.

How could I 'fix' this hole? If I didn't get out of bed at the time Bob did, I just didn't get out of bed. Silence, there is that wretched silence again; the silence after the storm, the hurricane! The silence turns into raw pain like a lemon in a fresh cut. It was just that this was more than a cut. It was a bottomless pit, sour and dark, like a cesspool. The body became so heavy that getting out of bed seemed to be too much work. I stayed there for a while, until the fear hit me. What if I end up in this bed with a bottle of vodka and say 'my baby' forever? I need to get out of here.

Kristina had been dead for six weeks when I 'celebrated' one year of sobriety Jan.15 1991. My body still showed signs of having been pregnant. There just was no baby. I could still 'feel' her on my left shoulder. There was that warm soothing sensation that spread up my neck and into my chest. My heart, oh how it hurt. Actually, the whole body hurt. When the sensation took over, I could not take it anymore, stuck a towel in my mouth, and crawled into the fetal position. I did that a lot.

I don't know how Bob got through it. I saw him cry once, after we handed back the cold towels to the nurse and sat in our private room. *Bob!! You just lost your daughter... if you don't cry now; there is something seriously wrong with you!* He took a minute, dropped a tear, swallowed, and that was it! Being the soldier he was, crying meant you let your emotions run you, and soldiers don't do that. That's for weak people. Bob was not weak! His heart had its challenges; but not Bob.

The year before Kristina was born Bob had felt some shortness of breath. He was only 37, so it could not be too serious. We had just married. Who wants to think about heart problems? After the angiogram, the verdict was quadruple bypass. We had some disagreements and settled for five angioplasties stretched over eighteen months. Bob would have an angioplasty done, go back to his life; after three, four months, the angina would reappear and back to the hospital he would go. He never spoke about it! After the fifth time, the doctor said, "..if you come in again, I'll open you up!" That was enough to quit the cigarettes. Bob figured he'll be on one table, having surgery, while I'll be on another having a baby.

It's an interesting situation to be pregnant and have your husband *dying*. It becomes even more interesting when your husband gets well and your baby dies! The 'considerate' people told me the solution, reminding me that I 'can always have more' like puppies! You need to get busy! Go to school, have another baby, get a job, but for God sake... don't think about it, time will heal all! Time does not heal it all. The body knows and remembers everything, forever until you are willing to feel and release. I did what others told me and got pregnant. I always did what others told me.

As a result, in 1992, Anna, daughter number two arrived. She had a rough entry into this world. She had been in a womb of tension, fear, anxiety, and rage on a daily basis. One second, I cursed out God, the next I was on the floor in the fetal position. She didn't have a chance for a *normal childhood*. Being Eva's baby set her up for some serious challenges. There was seldom a secure safe space for her to grow in.

I did not hit her. I *just* screamed and snapped, constantly. There is another loaded word: *just*. What we '*just*' do to our children has the potential to scar them for life; '*just*' does not make it any less damaging.

I could not figure out how to calm down. My body felt like it was going to explode, with a million mosquitoes under my skin, like low electrical currents shooting through my body. I felt weird vibrations trembling inside me. Like the day I came home from *the sleep over party* that August. I had turned fourteen in April 1972. All the motorcycle drivers planned on drinking until passing out, so we slept over.

My twenty-three-year-old boyfriend had a sleeping bag for both of us. What was I doing with a twenty-three-year-old boyfriend? "*Take your clothes off so we can share the body heat*," he said. That felt a little weird, but I was his girlfriend, so I did what he told me. I always did what I was told... by anyone.

Dory said I had not been shown how to say no, or how to set healthy boundaries. Boundaries, saying no; what is that? I said no, at age eight when the boys pulled my pants down and *examined* me. They still did it. I said no when my *rescuer* threw the boys out and wanted to be paid for the *protection*. He still did it. I said no when our neighbor upstairs wanted *a favor*. He locked the door and gave me *the look*, and still did it.

I was primed to offer no fight when my older boyfriend wanted to 'break in' yet another virgin. I whispered no, it hurt so much. "*It is suppose to,*" he said. I said it a little louder, but he still did it.

Mom was busy in the kitchen when I tried to tell her. I ended up telling her... twenty-two years later because mom was too busy. After three years with Dory, in 1994, I came home to my high school reunion. It was eight years since my last visit with mom. I felt strong enough to tell her. Her response should not have been a surprise, but it was. She said, "I don't remember that, it's so long ago... what were you doing there anyway... were you drinking? Don't you think it's time to be over that one... why do you have to dig into the old stuff anyway?"

Dory said that my Grandmother saved me, that she was probably the one who gave me enough love and attention to keep me going. I saw her in the summers. Mom had to leave me with "Mormor" to go back and finish school. I was 18-months-old the first time. One day, mom was just not there, saying that she had no choice. Mom was gone until I was three, and then one day, there she was again! I don't remember much. I just know, in my gut, that that was not a good thing. I have no memories of engaging in loving moments with Mom where I felt important or even wanted, although, I wonder if she ever got that from her mom. Sometimes I wonder if my girls feel like they get that from me.

I used to take Anna with me to Dory. I was too panicked to leave her with anybody. She was born with many challenges, but one kept me awake and alert and willing to be by her side at all times: Apnea. She would stop breathing, without warning, and I would have to 'kick start' her by tapping her 'all so gently' on the back, and pray! I knew she was going to die, I just didn't know when.

Dory pointed out that the problem with my wild, negative imagination was that what I feared could happen. I stayed within the possible, which made it difficult for Dory to 'logically' pull me out of it. All she could say was that maybe I was wrong. What if Anna lived to be old and I missed the opportunity to be with her because of fear. I'd ask, "*What do you mean, be with her? I am with her every day*"!

Dory said, "Be *present* with her."

There was that word again, *present*. They used to talk about being present in the program to help me stop drinking. I didn't really get that. When Kristina had died, I was told to stay present with the pain. The stepping-stone to spiritual growth was pain. You know what; you can have your spirituality. There were enough people in the meetings to 'dump' on. All these wonderful people that wanted to help took me for coffee and they listened... for hours! I was so self-absorbed I didn't appreciate or even thank them for their time. I just talked about me, myself, and Eva! The illnesses of Narcissism, what a lonely disease... *dis-ease*. I call it an illness; you end up alone while you make others ill.

I had not brought Anna to Dory after she turned one. I wanted to, but Dory claimed it was a way for me to divert attention and not be willing to look at the real issues. I didn't have issues. I had big 'holes' in my body that vibrated and ached, with no memories attached. It was strange to hear how others had all kinds of memories of their childhood; I could not remember a thing before I was about six, or maybe eight. I remember Dad, the captain of a big ship, who was home twice a year. I remember sitting on his lap, while he watched the horse races. He smelled of whiskey and cigarettes. Maybe I was seven. Next time I saw him I was thirteen. Mom had left him to marry a doctor. I was to go and visit my *father*. He had a few drinks, most days, and had his own way of teaching me about life. It is all a blur with pictures I don't want to be true.

In 1993 I was pregnant again. My OB/Gyn said, "No more children for at least two years! Your body has been through enough for now; two kids in two years and you are over thirty. But, she did not understand what I knew. In my gut I knew that we could not leave Anna alone with me. I knew I was crazy, ready for her to die, overwhelmingly controlling. I knew I would suffocate her if I did not have something else to divert my attention to. I knew children should have siblings. I knew - in my truth - children should not be left alone in the world.

It feels strange, almost funny to say that. I got a brother when I was four. I have very little memories about being with him. We were left alone in our apartment when mom worked, I was six and my brother was two. I looked at my girls around that age and felt sick. How could she leave us? My brother has memories being with me and Mormor, I just don't remember him. Dory said, it's because what happened to me so early in life. We tend to numb out and 'forget', the brains way of making it bearable to live. Guess what...the body remembers!!

When Maja came along I refused to take her home without a sleep study to see if she had Apnea, too. The specialists said: – It never happens twice in the same family. You can take her home. *Well, give her the study, or keep her here.* Maja had Apnea; another year of tense alertness... always.

It is interesting how Apnea controls your life. If I had to run down to change the laundry, I had to connect Anna or Maja to the monitor. Then I'll look at the time, run down to the garage, and throw the laundry in the drying, put the quarters in and get back up. There wasn't time for a new load, which had to be a separate trip. If the monitor would be beeping I'll look at the time and know how long she's been out of oxygen. I knew four minutes created brain damage so the trip shouldn't be more than one minute long; it took a few seconds to 'start her up again'. There was some embarrassment involved when it happened outdoors. I would walk down the street, staring at my child, and when she would stop breathing, I would loose it. Sometimes I screamed: breathe!! And people would turn around. Sometimes, all I could do was to 'pat her so gently' holding my own breath. I never got used to it.

Balancing Your Chemistry

I had met Rhonda in 1994. A friend of mine, Debi...one of the few who could tolerate my mood swings...or stand my narcissism, introduced us. That started the work of chemical recovery. In my perception, anybody that has 'pickled' their brain in alcohol has a chemical imbalance. I feel such a love and gratitude for Rhonda. She was working with people that had tried 'everything' and were so sick. She helped them back to life by balancing their chemistry through 'glandular therapy'.

I was so unpredictable, so volatile, and so tense, with mood swings nobody could truly understand, except for Rhonda. She would talk about how the body worked 'like a pond', and that you had to *balance your chemistry*. I was out of balance alright, I just didn't understand how 'being out of balance' could get me so imprisoned by my own mind. The world was the way I saw it! I didn't have the ability to 'be flexible', or interested in others, or even care. I cared about one thing; I needed to keep the babies alive! If it wasn't for Rhonda I would be on heavy dosages of something... psychotic... bi-polar... depressant... call it whatever you want... but I am not!! Because of Rhonda I have a life and an ability to feel life. It wasn't always easy to 'do the work' but it was the only way for me and without drugs!

One day in 1995 I told Anna to pick up her toys. She said no. I remember it as if I watch a movie, how I picked her up and threw her into her bed. A picture flashed by. I saw Anna's neck snap! I fell down and went into yet another panic attack. They were coming about 3-4 times/week. I knew how to put a towel in my mouth and hide the scream from the girls.

The next day I stormed into Dory's office; I need something, why can I not have Prozac or *something*? Half of those I know in treatment are on Prozac, why have you not prescribed it for me! I am going out of my mind. I think I'm a danger to my girls, for God sake, Dory. Yesterday I thought I killed Anna. What if I kill my children!?

Learning to Deal With the Weather

Her answer set me on a course to recovery that has been the hardest but most rewarding journey. She said, "..if I give you Prozac, I give you an umbrella. You will not feel the rain, but you will not feel the sunshine, either."

Wow, I got it! And if I closed the umbrella, I still wouldn't have figured out how to deal with the weather. I knew I was screwed. I knew, again, in my gut, that I needed to learn how to 'deal with the weather' without an umbrella. Now, Rhonda's work became the only way out of my rigid, imprisoned mind and body.

I had not had a drink for five years. I had had three children, and got to keep two of them. Bob's heart was doing fine. I knew it was just a matter of time when one of them would die. I had to be prepared! The tension was overwhelming and I snapped on a daily basis. Rhonda's work had started to show results but I had a long way to go. I had 'pickled' my brain for 17 years. It was going to take some time.

My husband was not 'available'. Being a soldier and having been brought up in an 'emotionally absent' household he was not skilled in 'being emotionally there.' But, he was there, went to work, and provided a lifestyle for his family that allowed me to be home with the girls. But, maybe I should have gone to work. Maybe that would have given the girls a break. They needed a break!

I started Anna in preschool. I knew I was suffocating her and she needed to get away from me. Maja was 1 ½ and had not received any individual attention so far. Anna was 'running' from morning to night, and Maja got to sit on my hip chasing Anna around. Research tells us how 'vital' it is for normal development for the child to have a secure attachment to their caregiver who should 'gaze into the infant eyes with a smile' and connect, so the child can feel secure. Gaze into the infants eyes... I would stare panicky to see if they were breathing...long after the Apnea was gone. Why didn't anybody tell me? It must have been obvious! Maybe if someone would have told me I was abusive, I would have 'awakened' sooner.

Breathe and Release

Adva had a daughter in the same preschool. She took one look at me and said I needed to breathe. She told me that if I learned how to breathe and release, my anxiety would be lessened. Anxiety... how did she know? Its funny how people 'know' you are out of your mind, but they just don't tell you. Adva was the first person who watched me with the girls and had enough guts to tell me I was hurting my children. "You need to calm down," she would say.

I knew that; I just didn't know how. My friends in recovery told me to pray more and to help another alcoholic. I was on my knees every morning, *please God; help me not to hurt my children today. Please Kristina, help me be a real mother. Help me take care of your little sisters today.*

I would get off my knees and the shaking and itching would start, the heat would rise in my stomach, the pressure would build in my chest, my arm and legs would shake. The rest of the day was spent trying to figure out how not to explode. All I could focus on was how to not scream, or cry, or do something that would scare the girls. But over and over again, I would scare the girls.

You know, sorry doesn't mean a thing. After the second time it gets watered down and after that you might as well not say it at all. Change the behavior that hurts others! Walk your talk!! I spent the next six years with Adva learning how to 'walk my talk'. Slowly I started to 'deal with the weather'. While Rhonda was helping my chemistry, Adva was helping me to breathe. She taught me how to breathe... just breathe through the shakes, through the boys attack, my 'protector's' demands. Just breathe... through the rape.

Rape is such a strange word. The dictionary says: 'The crime of forcing another person to submit to sex acts, especially sexual intercourse'. Mmm, if that was all, it would not have been so bad. How about the crime of drilling a hole into a woman's body and mind so that she becomes incapable of recognizing abuse even when it's glaring into her face? How about the crime of peeling off the inside of a woman's heart and soul, so that she is left with a ripped integrity and incapable of recognizing self-worth or self-respect?

Without those two ingredients in your character, you are doomed as I was to live a life of repetition of abuse and trauma like in the movie Groundhog Day. Truly, I would wake up without wanting to wake up, hoping it was just a dream, and today would be different. The rape set me up for another 17 years of Groundhog Days; violence... the perpetrator's name changed yet the story was the same.

By the time I got to America in 1983, I was 25; a woman with an emotional IQ of an eight-year-old girl; ripped of any sense of worth, desperately trying to stay numb; and primed for more abuse. I got more! This one was the dangerous type, bank robber, drug dealer, and wife beater. I actually married this one. I became his ninth wife. 'Your wife cannot testify against you' was an old law that ran Jack's decisions to marry every woman he spent time with. Once again, I did what I was told and married. It could make me legal in America.

Recognize the facts, they told me, it always gets worse!! Funny, how everybody knew...just that I didn't see how that applied to me. After five years with Jack there wasn't much left of me. "If you didn't make me so angry, I wouldn't have to beat you," he would say. I would think... how can I not make him so mad? Never would I have a thought go through my mind that he shouldn't beat me in the first place. How do we sink that low? I couldn't hit back... too risky I was told. And again, I did what I was told. I had been well-conditioned to do what I was told!

But one day he had 'that look' again and came toward me. Something snapped inside, I waved my arm and landed an elbow in his eye. He dropped me and the time stopped, I felt nothing, I was ready, to go. There was a weird feeling in the air, he stared me down. I had no fear, no shakings, numb, as if I wasn't even there at all. It was an amazing feeling, nothingness! How I wanted that nothingness. *Go ahead Jack*. He didn't; it wasn't worth another trip to jail.

Bob did not believe in beating women. He was my next-door neighbor and best friend. I had one rule that you do not sleep with your best friend. We had been friends for about a year the first time he got the pleasure of meeting my ex-husband, Jack. I needed Jack for my green card; the process had never been completed. I had let him stay on the couch; after all, he was doing me a favor. It was midnight when he came into my room and I screamed for Bob to come. When I was knocked down, this time I felt something, like a pilot light, a flicker of Eva. Bob came to my rescue. It was the first time I had experienced protection without a price tag, a friend being there for me, just because. What a strange but wonderful feeling. He has been there ever since. We married in October 1989.

It took 15 years before Bob started to 'engage'. After countless fights, dramas, threats, and begging he found it possible to 'open up'. Although, who can blame him. Living with a delusional wife who would change moods on a dime can make a 'clam' out of anybody. I guess he needed his Military Ranger skills to be able to endure, and he endured a lot!

I could go off without any warning. I would get a feeling, start to shake, my mind would 'scan for a reason' and most often land on Bob or the girls, and off I would go. I truly believed they were the reason for how I felt, so if I could control them, I would feel better, wouldn't I? Wasn't that how it worked? Jack told me I made him mad... I told Bob and the girls that they made me mad, and on and on we would go.

Where do we learn how to be, if we don't get it from home? How many years are wasted by not knowing how to live? How can we teach our children what we don't know? Few could be around me long enough to get to know me. They told me in recovery that I was not bad, just very sick. I don't know... being a sick person didn't sound that good either.

Transformation Begins

In 2001, I was told I should become a Life Coach. I had had such a miserable life and seemed to be pretty recovered, why not help others? So, once again I did what I was told and went to coaching school. That was the first time I was introduced to Eva, not the alcoholic, not the victim, not the survivor, not the ...whatever!! I thought I knew something, after 11 years in recovery from alcoholism I must have learned something. Yes, to talk about my 'story' over and over again. That year I had my guts ripped out by another process; a series of self-development 'tools' that introduced me to Eva the Narcissist.

When it dawned on me that I only thought about myself; my children had to live, so *I* wouldn't have any bad feelings. My husband had to live, so *I* could feel good. Everything was about how *I* felt and what *I* thought. I was so embarrassed and so humiliated when I realized how I must have looked to the world. New Ventures West taught me how to grow up.

Part of my training program was to do Yoga, Bikram yoga. In my life experience this was the most ridiculous exercise to go through; actually ridiculously painful. To have to look at yourself in a mirror, standing in the 'most ridiculous' posture looking at the 'gorgeous' people, comparing myself... be clumsy... ugly... not perfect; and having to feel all my feelings that would come up, without being allowed to leave, scream, or talk. To have to watch my mind take off in the most frightening ways with thoughts I don't even want to admit to myself. To have to watch and feel my mind and body without moving, only breathing, was excruciating! I have done Yoga ever since. After two years it started to become 'easier' and now I don't want to live without it.

So, now I was a coach. I still felt like a fake, my mood swings were more bearable, not as violent, but I still was not that pleasant to be around. I read the book, <u>Awakening the Tiger</u> with Peter Levine. It talked about trauma and survivors of trauma. There were fourteen characteristics of a trauma survivor. I had all but two! I grabbed a towel and curled into fetal position. Here I was. This is what's wrong with me. They offered a three year Somatic Experience training program. My whole body said yes! I had to do this.

Today there is hope.

The Somatic Experience training has been a trying process of, once again, going through my life, this time with my body. I am now 50! I have learned how to release the pain, the pressures, and shakings. My body is starting to feel like *home*. It is actually possible to live with *me* today. Possible for me, and for my family!

Bob has 'been there' now for 18 years. He is a stable rock, the anchor in our family. We communicate because we can! Bob and I never had a honeymoon; we 'just didn't have time'. Now we finally do - a long one!

I owe so much to the women in my life that saw what I could not see; the human being inside of this shell. A few friendships are left, who kept me going, Debi, Adva, Rhonda, and new ones are forming, who keep me aware and awake. Helen, Meg and a few more in progress are helping. Thank you, ladies for being you; and thank you for allowing me to be me. They say humans are social animals and without others we die. I was dying; I just didn't know.

Today, 2008, Anna is sixteen and Maja is fourteen, the most beautiful girls on this planet. How they are dealing with life is magical to watch. They made it through, miraculously. I don't know how much damage I've done. On a good day I feel they have great support and will make it. On a bad day, I crumble into fetal position and grab my towel.

I have at last been shown a way to live in my body and mind, in the present moment! I can be with people today and treasure relationships.

Eva, welcome home! It took almost fifty years! I don't take drugs, I am so grateful for my full range of emotions and sensations. Today I am alive, and quite capable of dealing with the weather.

Eva Angvert Harren is an Integral Coach. Her expertise is centered in the areas of Somatic Self-Awareness and Body-Mind Stress Management. Working with Eva will guide you to intuitively know how your "felt sense" and addictions impinge on your behaviors and sense of wellbeing. This awareness benefits all areas of your lives and results in more successful Integrative Behaviors and Communication Skills, which leaves you feeling more competent, successful and whole. Eva works with individuals, groups, and corporations helping people realize and develop their power within.

Phone: 510.825.7574 angvert@beam-intl.com or visit her on the web at www.beam-intl.com

Never Alone
Jenna Kandyce Linch

I found myself actually sitting in my room thinking about my past. This poem originated from that. Sometimes when I find myself stressed out and feeling kind of down and out about things, I think about how far I have come in my life and how much further I have yet to go. I also know that I have so many friends who are there for me and have stood beside me through all the hard times.

I've had to fight hard to get this far but I know that never again will I go back to the victim role. My life is not ending; it is just beginning for me.

Never Alone

She sits alone, staring at the blank walls

Inside for someone to listen her heart calls.

Back down memory lane she's gone

In her mind, past memories play on.

Revisiting her past, she's taken to days of long ago

Things that she never wanted anyone to know.

For the path she once traveled was very dark

That part of her life became a dangerous part on which to embark.

As she looks back, she sees the wreckage of her life's chaos

Stolen innocence was her greatest loss.

All these years the haunting memories she's tried to suppress

Because she feared that of her people would think less.

Nothing happened were the words she learned to recite

Yet everyday home turned into a battlefield where she had to fight.

Often she found herself trapped on the warpath

Feeling the pain left from the aftermath.

With no one there to protect her, herself she had to defend

Threatened into silence, that everything was fine she was forced to pretend.

This little girl grew up faster than one could imagine

But with her remained the scars of sin.

A dark period of her life she entered

To some of the toughest times she encountered to them she referred.

She found herself dangerously close to defeat

Into depression and self-infliction she did retreat.

Brainwashing was her abusers' weapon of choice

For they did not want her to use her voice.

Her self-esteem became greatly marred

Looking at her reflection, she saw an image emotionally scarred.

Love in her life was non-existent

The girl nobody wanted, away she got sent.

She watched her life spiral out of control

As the effects of the damage done took its toll.

All alone, many tears she cried

But those tears from everyone else she learned to hide.

The burden of shame and guilt that was not hers she bore

As into a million pieces her heart tore.

Her heart bleeds as she recalls the hate and violence

Just thinking about it makes her grow tense.

Exactly how she survived it she couldn't say how

Yet the pain from the past lingers on, even now.

Much of her life she felt very isolated

Being a trapped victim she hated.

She was viewed as different because of her history

Beyond her past people chose not to see.

All of this she thinks about as she sits alone tonight

The miracle is that she lived because she decided to fight.

Yes, she could have quit and thrown her life away

Strong-willed and stubborn, she chose in life to stay.

It took time for her to learn to love herself

Especially when for years her heart was on a shelf.

What she was made of she found

Discovering the strength within, she stood her ground.

What keeps her going is knowing her life holds so much more

Everyday as she pieces her heart together, hope and faith she's able to restore.

With the world, her story, she shares

Letting others out there know there's someone who cares.

So tonight, she walks out of that empty room, leaving her past behind

That she's not going to give up she made up her mind.

Like a Phoenix, she rises above the ashes of her past

For she plans on rebuilding a life foundation that will last.

Even though she's been through a lot, she knows she's where she's suppose to be

Of her survival, her scars are her testimony.

Because of her experiences, into a stronger woman she's grown

Now wherever she goes, she brings the message that no one is ever alone.

'Never Alone' Copyright © Jenna Kandyce Linch

Jenna Kandyce Linch *is a Poet and advocate whose life's devotion is to helping others.*

Candalyse Publishing
is an independent publishing company that
publishes books to enlighten, inspire, and uplift its readers.
We publish stories of real people who have chosen to use their
inspirational life stories to empower others.

For more information about our company please visit:

www.candalysepublishing.com
candalysepublishing@gmail.com

We believe in delivering the highest quality products and services. Our clients are our greatest asset and we are dedicated to serving their needs.

Please Visit Us on The Web

Miriam L. Jacobs was inspired to compile the ten volume inspirational series, *How to Jump from a Ferris Wheel and Land on Your Feet*, as she sought additional ways to empower and inspire others. Mrs. Jacobs is a Mother, Grandmother, Author, Publisher, Life Coach, Inspirational Speaker, and Mentor. who has devoted her life to encouraging others to be the best that they can be despite life's annoying obstacles. . She is in recovery for nineteen years from Alcoholism and for six years from Chronic Depression, as well as a survivor of Domestic Violence. A percentage of every sale goes towards her granddaughter's facial reconstructive surgeries. Candace Battiste was born with a very rare skin disorder known as Giant Congenital Nevus.

For more information please visit http://www.NOI.org

Candace
Believe in Miracles
imikimi.com

To purchase the Ferris Wheel Series please visit:

www.ferriswheelseries.faithweb.com

Bulk volume discounts are available for

- **Churches and Synagogues**

- **Teen crisis Centers**

- **Substance Abuse Treatment Facilities**

- **Women's Outreach Organizations**

- **Ministries**

- **Corporations**

- **Domestic Violence Centers**

- **And more...**

Contact the Publisher

If you or someone you know, would like to share an inspirational chapter from your life in a future volume in the Ferris Wheel Series, please contact Miriam L. Jacobs, Founder Candalyse Publishing.

Candalyse Publishing

PO Box 783 Smallwood, New York 12778

Printed in the United States
206230BV00002B/1-105/P